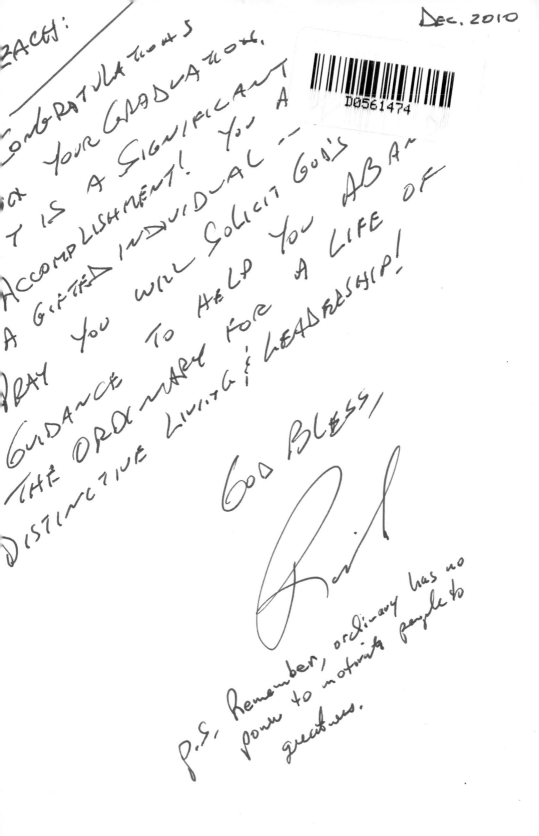

ZACH:

DEC. 2010

CONGRATULATIONS

or YOUR GRADUATION.

IT IS A SIGNIFICANT

ACCOMPLISHMENT! YOU A

A GIFTED INDIVIDUAL --

I PRAY YOU WILL SOLICIT GOD'S

GUIDANCE TO HELP YOU ABAN

THE ORDINARY FOR A LIFE OF

DISTINCTIVE LIVING & LEADERSHIP!

GOD BLESS,

P.S. Remember, ordinary has no
power to motivate people to
greatness.

ABANDON
THE
ORDINARY

ABANDON
THE
ORDINARY

Building a Distinctive Leadership Brand
in Business, Family, and Church

RICHARD S. LYTLE

Abilene, Texas

ABANDON THE ORDINARY

Building a Distinctive Leadership Brand in Business, Church, and Family

Copyright 2010 by Richard S. Lytle

First Edition

Publication of this book has been supported by a gift from James R. Porter. Thank you.

ISBN 978-0-89112-541-9

Printed in the United States of America

All Scripture quotations taken from The Holy Bible, New International Version. Copyright 1984, International Bible Society. Used by permission of Zondervan Publishers.

Cover design by Jeanette Munger
Interior text design by Sandy Armstrong

For information contact:
Abilene Christian University Press
1626 Campus Court
Abilene, Texas 79601
1-877-816-4455
www.abilenechristianuniversitypress.com

10 11 12 13 14 15 16 / 7 6 5 4 3 2 1

Dedication

To Gram and Pop:
matriarch and patriarch of our family faith.

To Frank and Lois Lytle:
a silent force for God.

To Bill and Jim Lytle:
brothers who loved me and cared for me before I was aware.

To Kelly, Hannah, and Michelle:
given to me out of all the daughters in heaven—three of my greatest blessings. I am proud of you and will love you for always. Be there!

To Jeanne:
your love, friendship, beauty, talent, kindness, service, encouragement, and godly example have blessed my life, shaping me for eternity. I love you deeply.

Acknowledgments

I wish to thank my good friend and college roommate, Mark Kirk, for his foundational contributions to this work years ago. His thoughts on leadership and power have greatly influenced many of my students as well as my own thinking and development. The final sections of this book are underpinned by his ideas. Thank you friend!

Also, I wish to offer thanks to Heidi Nobles and Greg Taylor. Greg, thanks for cutting and shaping my manuscript early on while being kind to a rookie author. Heidi, thanks for managing the final stages, performing more textual surgery, staying on task, and refining the manuscript into a significantly better work. And, special thanks to Dr. C. Leonard Allen, director of ACU Press, for believing in me and in this project.

Finally, I wish to thank those who, beyond family, have had significant spiritual influence on my life: Will Ed and Mickey Warren, Vernon and Alice Boyd, Silas and Edna Mae Shotwell, Steve and Jane Watson, Jack and Ann Griggs, Terry and Gayla Pope, Monty and Libby Lynn, Gary and Millie Skidmore and the Hallal Board, Bill and Donna Petty, Johnny and Rosemary Stites, and Dwayne and Joan VanRheenen. Last but not least, special thanks and adoration to my two buddies who have joined me in my work at ACU and stood by me through thick and thin: Tim Johnston and Mike Winegeart—strength and honor!

Table of Contents

Introduction

As a leader you want to distinguish yourself from the crowd. You do not want to be ordinary. You know the world needs distinctive leaders more than ever, but such people are in short supply.

Why? Some are afraid; others are selfish. Some are adrift on the sea of life, bobbing up and down in the swells and battered by the winds.

What about you? Do you desire distinction in leadership? If you do, you must abandon the ordinary life and chart a course using godly coordinates set on eternal goals.

I grew up in Michigan around the Great Lakes. The Great Lakes soaked into my soul, instilled a deep love of, and appreciation for, water, boats, and lighthouses. The Great Lakes are clear, cold, and deep—very deep—parts of Lake Superior are more than one thousand feet deep. The lakes, wide and long, span hundreds of miles from end to end. For fifty consecutive summers, I have been blessed to visit these waters, interact with them, ride on them, swim in them, ski on them, and marvel at them.

God has revealed himself to me in these lakes. Like the millions who play and engage in commerce on the lakes, I love these magnificent and complex waters. I'm telling you about this part of my life because I want to share a leadership principle from these waters as we begin.

Abandoning the ordinary and building a leadership brand that matters is like captaining a ship. As I've captained boats on the Great Lakes and watched others navigate, I've discovered what Don Soderquist, former vice chairman of Walmart, says is true about great leaders: they are like great captains. How do they compare?

Good captains chart a great course. The best captains are familiar with the best destinations and they know how to plot and navigate a course for safe arrival. In the same way, good leaders know the way. They know what is best about life and they have the ability to plot a successful course for a particular business, church, or family, navigating well for safe arrival.

Good captains know about hidden danger. Some dangers en route are sub-surface and are not indicated on the charts. Nevertheless, a good captain knows they exist and he steers clear of them, bringing his ship to safe harbor. Likewise, good leaders maintain an awareness of the dangers that exist, and they know how to steer clear of these dangers for those entrusted to them.

Good captains are steady at the helm. They don't unnecessarily cause the ship to pitch and roll, endangering and upsetting passengers. They change course only when necessary and in a way that passengers and crew are not unduly upset in the process. In similar fashion, a good leader is not constantly creating unnecessary change. She understands that change is difficult and upsetting for most. Thus, she steers with caution and prudence.

Good captains visit passengers and crew. The captain visits the engine room, the deck, the galley, and the living quarters, gaining insight into the condition of the operation. In order to do this, he must entrust the ship's direction to a second officer who can handle the job. Good leaders, too, get out among their people and their operations. They inspect the condition of the unit and get to know the people, seeing them at work. However, they must be able to entrust the ongoing operations of the business or church to someone who is second in command.

Good captains and leaders must handle emergencies well. In the midst of crisis, they must respond with knowledge, decisiveness, and tenacity. It has been said that emergencies don't create character; they display it. Thus, those who are well prepared prosper.

Abandon the Ordinary is written to help you captain your ship, lead with passion, and leave generic living and leadership behind. Do you have what it takes to lead your family, your team, your church, or your company? *Abandon the Ordinary* describes what it takes and guides you toward charting a course that builds a distinctive brand of leadership that matters.

There's one other thing you should know before we go further on this journey.

Leadership starts with God and our closest relationships on earth. I love God and cherish my family as a divine gift from him. It is the first place where I learn and model distinctive leadership. My wife, Jeanne, and I are blessed to have three exceptional daughters (Kelly, Hannah, Michelle) who have helped us define God's brand of leadership for our family. When they were young, we began our family's leadership journey by explaining that God's brand of leadership meant getting MAD (making a difference) for Jesus! Our initial framework was an outcropping of Micah 6:8:

> Act justly.
> Love mercy.
> Walk humbly with the Lord.

When the girls were elementary age, we discovered they could recite the source of our family mission—but had no clue as to what it meant. So, in order to chart the right course and help them captain their own ships, we had them memorize Micah 6:8 using the LIV (Lytle Innovative Version) text.

First, we taught them that "act justly" meant always **do the right thing**. We explained that people often do the wrong thing. However, as leaders for God, they were always to do the right thing.

Second, we taught them that "love mercy" means to **love forgiveness**. They should love receiving forgiveness and love giving it to others. We explained that many people don't forgive. However, as leaders for God, they are to pass forgiveness all around.

Finally, we taught them that "walk humbly with God" means to **remember you are not God**. We explained that oftentimes all of us begin to live as if we were God and that everything revolves around us. However, as leaders for God, we are to remember that God is supreme and powerful and that we are to obey his will.

The world needs great leaders. But how do you build a leadership brand that matters?

Your ability to lead with power in a complex global society will largely depend on your ability to move away from a generic type of leadership. The farther you move your life from generic, the more powerful and influential you become. If your brand of leadership is not valued by people, you will not be a leader. In other words, your brand of leadership must have a value proposition that connects with a massive, yet flat, global society that increasingly embraces conflicting and competing interests and value systems.

Therefore, building a brand of leadership that matters will be the result of abandoning the ordinary while understanding and managing four fundamental "P"s that comprise the genetic fabric of God's leadership brand: Perspective, Position, Power, and Promise. From Adam to Abraham to Moses to David to Esther to Mary to Jesus to Paul to YOU, leadership brands that matter are built upon these fundamental elements.

This book creates a godly blueprint for you to strategically manage the four "P"s. The effective understanding and management of these will underpin a process of moving quickly away from ordinary and becoming a branded and distinctive leader among those you love and lead.

The first section of the book examines how your perspective frames the foundation for building your brand.

The second section explores how you can assess your God-given positions in life and make them the focus of your earthly work.

The third section investigates the nature of power and how harnessing real power in life builds the brand on a daily basis.

Finally, the fourth section shows how you can create, deliver, and manage a distinctive set of promises with the personal signature of gifts and positions God has given you.

An Invitation

I'm humbled that building a brand of leadership that matters is not my choice but a privilege and call from God. For some, this realization causes great angst. For me, it is exhilarating and motivational. What about for you?

My daughter, Michelle, has always enjoyed the thrill of a call over the intercom at school when I picked her up early for a special occasion. "Daddy," she says, "I always wait and hope that it will be my name that is called."

Our names have been called. We have been called out by our heavenly father who wants the best for us and from us! He wants to give us his brand and his mark of excellence for living and leadership. Indeed, Jesus says to us, "You did not choose me, but I chose you to go and bear fruit—fruit that will last."[1] That sounds like a signature brand of fruit. No doubt, it is requisite to the brand. The blood at the cross was not spilled for mediocrity to reign within us. Jesus through Peter said, "you are a chosen people, a royal priesthood, a holy nation, a people belonging to God, that you may declare the praises of him who called you out of darkness into his wonderful light. Once you were not a people, but now you are the people of God."[2] Max Lucado has said that God loves you just the way you are, but he refuses to leave you that way. Does this make you afraid? Consider a different course. His love and call provide a blueprint for living, hope, and a marvelous future.

Are you ready to weather the storms and captain the ship of your life, your family, and your organization? Are you ready to abandon—even run away from—the ordinary? That's the first step toward becoming God's brand of leader.

Part One

———

PERSPECTIVE

Chapter One

THE TROUBLE WITH GENERIC

To be evil is to trivialize your life
and make ordinary that which God created.
It is to prostitute great potential for nothing.

—JIM McGUIGGAN

You've probably never heard of Al Williams or his company, but if you lived in the 1980s, you likely used products he created.

In the 1970s, Williams, a private label product lines manager at Albertsons Stores in Boise, Idaho, started a business. He introduced brand-less products to supermarkets and they came to be called "generic products."

During economic hardship, these products were marketed with a black and white label and simple description of the item: Cola.

Williams developed many products and the concept spread to many independent grocery stores and supermarket chains. An endless sea of black and white packages lined shelves. From soup to nuts, every product for sale looked the same. These black and white products were called *generic products* because there was no discernable difference in size, packaging, quality, or price. All were the same. All were cheap.

Consumers purchased these products using price as their primary decision-making variable. They were looking for the cheapest option and found thousands of them up and down these *generic* aisles. For several years, consumers witnessed a vast array of products without distinction.

Generic products seemed a great success! So why are black and white labels missing from grocer's shelves today? Because products without quality and distinction have little ability to create enduring value or influence. In virtually every product category worldwide, regardless of economic cycle (prosperity or decline), people have no lasting interest in that which is ordinary. The famous little girl holding the umbrella on the navy blue Morton salt container has won, and always will win, the dominant market share position because she is distinctively different.

This first and important principle holds true for God's brand of leadership. In the long run, *generic* living and leadership proves unattractive, holding little power to influence and create value for others. Leaders whose lives reflect quality and distinction, however, hold the power to create significant value and influence in others for change that really matters!

TABLE 1.1 Generic Brands vs. Distinctive Brands	
Generic Brands/Leaders	Distinctive Brands/Leaders
Undifferentiated	Distinct Set of Promises
Hold No Real Value	Highly Valuable
No Emotional Appeal	Connect with People
Powerless	Highly Influential
Not Managed Well	Managed Extremely Well
Short-lived	Enduring
Ultimate Failure	Successful

Unfortunately, research from George Barna and others suggests that *generic* best describes today's American brand of Jesus. As a brand of living displayed on the global shelves of humanity, there is often little discernable difference in its attributes, features, and promises from other lifestyles. Christian life for so many potential leaders is ordinary. As a brand, it is often marketed as a relatively cheap option, and thus the brand is losing growth and influence—it is rarely distinctively different. Thus, the "brand name" of Christ, the name for which he gave his life, is being devalued.

Many American Christian homes apparently embrace and reflect society's ultimate purpose, moral values, spending patterns, language use, media choices, activities, social habits, attitudes, and civic interest. They are undifferentiated, unmanaged, and often ultimately failures. In short, the brand name of Jesus gets a bad rap, holding no real value because these generic homes are made up of individuals holding no real power for change that really matters.

Similarly, many churches today are dying because they are generic, lacking any distinction from other social organizations. They reflect that which is easy and popular, stunting substantive and authentic spiritual development. These churches fail to connect with people, challenge people, and add little value to their personal lives. Thus, church members, representing the brand name of Christ to the world for 165 out of 168 hours per week, remain unchanged and ill-equipped to lead in a complex and dynamic society.

The reality is this: the modern church is losing its voice in the public square. It should be speaking powerfully to the moral challenges and brokenness of life in this world, applying the balm of truth and grace to wounds that are fresh and open, but it is not. It is adrift and *generic*. According to some, the American church has failed to pass on its faith to young people. Ironically, billions of dollars have been spent on youth ministries, Christian music, publishing, and media, producing a culture of young Christians who know next to nothing about God, his word, and their own faith except how they *feel* about it.[1] The result: declining membership in churches.

Recently, one of our daughters confirmed the void of true power in generic living and leadership. Upon her return from her first high school home Bible study, she explained that the youth group was studying the impact of environment and media on one's purity and spiritual development. At the conclusion of the study, the group leader stated that media such as music, television, internet, videos, and magazines had little, if any, impact on Christians. He told the kids that he usually listens to bad music, watches bad television and movies, and reads bad things, but he seemed to be okay.

This person's lack of awareness regarding the relationship between environment and personal development led to a missed opportunity to be a distinctive leader for the young people present. Upon reflection, she said she felt this leader didn't stand up for anything; she wanted more. In the long run, teens will tell you time and again, they are not interested in *generic*. Indeed, churches and youth groups witnessing explosive growth today are being led by individuals who teach and live drastically different lifestyles from those promoted in the world.

Dr. Bill Banowsky, former president of Pepperdine University and the University of Oklahoma, used to publicly pronounce, "It is a sin to be ordinary." His words express that *ordinary* is not a description of our calling from Jesus. "Average" hardly describes the life and leadership of our Savior. It should not describe ours. The purpose of Jesus was to live an *exemplary* life worthy of the calling he had received from his father in heaven.[2] Why? Because that type of living and leadership has the power to change what really matters.

Jesus' high calling inspired Dr. Martin Luther King, Jr. He called a generation away from *generic* living by using the word "exemplary" in his revolutionary speech to challenge the nation on civil rights issues. Exemplary is a medieval word meaning "to clear the way" or "to clear the forest."

The prophet Isaiah spoke to the purpose of God's brand of leadership when he said, "every valley shall be raised up, every mountain and hill made low; the rough ground shall become level, the rugged places a plain. And the glory of the Lord will be revealed, and all mankind together will see it."[3] In other words, the distinctive disciple of Jesus will build a brand of leadership that embraces a distinct set of promises, connects with people, and is managed so well that it will powerfully and dynamically clear a way for everyone to see God.

Trivializing your life to generic status is evil and sinful, according to Jim McGuiggan. He states, "to make ordinary that which God calls life and use your gifts and capacities for nothing is to prostitute great potential. Jesus Christ came into the world to convict us not so much of our transgressions but of our possibilities and to deliver us from an empty way of life." Again, McGuiggan says, "God must become ill at times when he sees us so trivial, so paltry, thinking such little things, when such great and honorable and glorious things are there in front of us."[4]

Common, average, or mediocre are never used to describe the ultimate work of God. When creation was finished, God declared it to be awesome! He was the passionate craftsman, pronouncing extraordinary satisfaction in his ultimate and completely satisfying work. He did not merely use the Hebrew word "good" (*tov*). He proclaims "very good" (*tov meod*) to describe the work of his hands.

The Purpose of a Brand

The earliest notions of the modern term "brand" were born on the prairies of America. Originally, the term brand described a rancher's burn or "mark" into a calf to identify it out of the many that roamed the prairies. The brand was a special mark or design owned by the rancher and used in registering his cattle and horses. Thus, branding was an essential and significant piece of daily work for the rancher. The handmade iron or steel tool that applied the mark to the horse or cow was called a branding iron. Once it was heated to a red hot condition, traditionally in a corral fire, the branding iron was pressed against the side of the animal.

Each of these iron designs was recorded in statewide brand books published by the respective Departments of Agriculture, which often provided the ultimate evidence of ownership in disputes. Even today, brand books provide illustrations of brands, list previous owners, and give the locations of the mark on the animals. To be sure, "branding 'Irons' are serious business."[5]

In a spiritual sense, God's "branding iron" is serious business, as well. His ultimate evidence of ownership is his mark on you and me, identifying us as his, out of the many that roam the prairies of life. Thus, developing and protecting his brand name matters! It is an essential and significant piece of daily work for God.

To Abram he said, "I will make you into a great nation" and "I will make your name great."[6] To Moses he said, "Out of all nations, you will be my treasured possession."[7] To King David he said, "I will make your name like the names of the greatest men of the earth"[8] and "For the sake of his great name, the Lord will not reject his people."[9]

Years ago, the greatest leadership brand alive was born. The masses traveled long distances to hear Jesus' brand of teaching. The poor cried when they witnessed his compassion. Sinners fell prostrate as they encountered his forgiveness and freedom. Evil fled his presence as he cleared the temple. Twelve men made their decision to follow when he washed their feet. Everyone in the room felt the press of his mark against their hearts that night. After three short years of ministry, they all knew the brand of God, and it mattered deeply.

More than two thousand years later, the brand endures. Today, the distinctive characteristics and traits that belong to his brand of leadership are the same as they were when he walked the dusty, worn streets of Galilee.

When God places his mark on you, you are branded for distinctive leadership—leadership that matters—set apart from the rest with a name, a mission, and power to move the masses. Because you are branded, you are not generic.

Early on, Israel looked and acted like its neighbors. God's brand was diluted and they lost their ability to create value and influence for the nations around them. In desperation, Moses cries out to God, "What else will distinguish me and your people from all the other people on the face of the earth?"[10]

God responds, "I will do the very thing you have asked, because I am pleased with you and I know you by name."

Then Moses said, "Now show me your glory."[11]

Moses asked to see the attributes and promises of the greatest leadership brand alive. God agreed to Moses's request and passed in front of him proclaiming, "The Lord, the Lord, the compassionate and gracious God, slow to anger, abounding in love and faithfulness, maintaining love to thousands, and forgiving wickedness, rebellion and sin. Yet he does not leave the guilty unpunished; he punishes the children and their children for the sin of the fathers to the third and fourth generations."[12]

So these are the brand promises of God:

Compassion
Love
Longsuffering
Faithfulness
Forgiveness
Justice
Holiness

These are not *generic* promises. These are promises, specific to his brand, that create the needed distinction to accomplish important and believable leadership among mankind.

At one time, God used the outward marks of circumcision, pillars of fire and clouds, tabernacles, and temples to identify the brand and those who belonged to him. However, in reality, he has always desired to make his mark by branding the hearts and minds of his followers.[13]

Jim Eliot's life was marked by the brand promises of God. In 1956, he took the gospel to the Auca Indians. As he got out of his canoe and walked toward their village, they shot him and fellow missionaries with dozens of razor-sharp arrows. He died within minutes.

In a journal, he had recorded a prayer that expressed his heart before he went to South America. He said; *"Father, make of me a crisis man. Bring those*

I contact to a point of decision. Let me not be a milepost on the road of their lives. Make me a fork in that road that men must turn one way or another when they face the Christ in me."

Eliot's brand promise cost him his life. His wife, though, also bore the brand, and she took the message of Jesus Christ to the same Indians who had killed her husband. The very men who took life from her husband later surrendered to Jesus and became missionaries themselves.[14] Jim's prayer was fulfilled. He *was* a fork in the road that made these men choose one way or the other when they encountered the brand of God.

Great Brands Come with Great Passion

Great brands exist because someone had the passion or desire to make them great.

The prevalence of "generic" exists primarily because it is easier to produce than excellence, according to Jim Collins: "Few people attain great lives, in large part because it is just so easy to settle for a good life."[15]

Truly, a brand of excellence is exceedingly difficult to produce. It requires energy, passion, resolve, and focus. Unfortunately, most people and most organizations don't even desire greatness and distinction, let alone work for it. Thus, they never achieve it. The watershed moment in an individual, family, or organization comes when someone discovers that *greatness and distinction* are possible and worthy of pursuit.

For Albert Pujols, moving from *generic* to a level of distinction began when he decided that greatness is worthy of pursuit and hard work. Pujols, first baseman for the St. Louis Cardinals and two-time National League MVP, is building a brand of leadership that matters through his passion, resolve, and focus. "I don't judge. Only God can judge," he says. "I've always had the responsibility to God to be a role model, so it's not just now. I play to represent God, something bigger than baseball. This is not about me. I leave everything up to God."[16] Pujols is building a distinctive brand!

Legendary basketball coach John Wooden long espoused that greatness and excellence are about making every effort to be the best *you* can be on a daily basis: "The effort must be total, and when it is . . . you have achieved personal success."[17] Wooden's philosophy built a brand of basketball heretofore unseen in NCAA athletics.

One day a couple of colleagues and I tried to persuade another colleague and good friend of mine at the university, Dr. Terry Pope, to skip his workout and join us for lunch.

With his gym bag slung over his shoulder, he turned to us, and said with exceptionally dry wit, "Great athletes work out. You need to decide if you want to be a great athlete." He smiled and walked past us. His words are axiomatic and as true as hot dust in a West Texas summer. The desire for greatness always precedes greatness itself. Terry could have quoted Aristotle, who said, "We are what we repeatedly do. Excellence, then, is not an act, but a habit."

A lot of research has shown that greatness is largely determined by desire and practice, not "innate gifting." Nobody is great without desire and hard work. "It's nice to believe that if you find the field where you're naturally gifted, you'll be great from day one, but it doesn't happen. There's no evidence of high-level performance without [desire,] experience or practice."[18]

So greatness and distinction aren't handed to anyone on a silver platter; these require a lot of hard work. The researchers above say that the best people in any field are those who have the desire to be great, which results in what they call "deliberate practice." This type of practice involves four elements:

1. Activity that is specifically intended to improve performance
2. Reaching for objectives just beyond one's level of competence
3. Obtaining and analyzing feedback on results
4. High levels of repetition

"Simply hitting a bucket of balls," the researchers say, "is not deliberate practice, which is why most golfers don't get better. Hitting an eight iron three hundred times with a goal of leaving the ball within twenty feet of the pin eighty percent of the time, continually observing results and making appropriate adjustments, and doing that for hours every day—that's deliberate practice."[19]

Can you imagine how our families might move toward greatness if we did the following?

1. Engage in strategies that are specifically intended to improve our family's performance.
2. Reach for family objectives beyond our current realm of competence.

3. Collect and analyze data about our families.
4. Engage in high levels of repetition regarding the things that really matter.

Families that deliberately practice these strategies would begin to be distinctive, building a brand of "family" that glorifies God and has the power to create value and influence for others.

Good enough never achieves greatness in anything! Greatness and distinction in life never has been, and never will be, marked by that which is ordinary. It was true of Jesus' life. It is true of yours. Great teaching is never a function of *ordinary* passion, preparation, and practice. Great learning is not accomplished with common inquisitiveness. Powerful lives are never a result of generic living. A strong desire for greatness coupled with hard work and deliberate practice achieves greatness in all aspects of living and leadership.

Families cannot achieve greatness in homes where parents embrace mediocrity. Likewise, great churches cannot experience prosperity and spiritual growth with run-of-the-mill vision and leadership. And I must tell you that salvation was not secured with an attitude of "good enough." Salvation required desire, hard work, and deliberate practice because the brand mattered!

Promise Management

In essence, a brand is a promise. Throughout time, the brand's greatness is underpinned by its ability to consistently make good on a set of compelling and distinctive promises. Over time, its value and influence are built upon the management and daily implementation of those brand promises.

Our local high school track coach gets this principle. Every athlete that participates on his team signs a statement promising to represent the school with excellence and pride in speech, conduct, example, and performance. If not, discipline will result. Coach believes it is a privilege to be a part of the team and he wants students who are interested in building the brand name of his program. Sounds familiar, doesn't it?

Check out "Coach Paul's" advice to young Timothy as a leader and brand builder in ancient times: "set an example for the believers in speech, in life, in love, in faith, and in purity."[20]

In the global marketplace, the brand promise is pre-eminent. For instance, Walmart's promise has always been to deliver low prices to customers. Today, they express the promise in the words "Save money. Live better." Lexus guarantees the relentless pursuit of perfection in the design and manufacture of its automobiles. Steve Jobs and the folks at Apple pledge innovation and design for customers. And for more than 110 years, the J. M. Smucker name has been among the most recognized brands in America with their enduring promise, "with a name like Smuckers, it has to be good."

In 1897, Jerome Smucker sold his first product—apple butter—from the back of a horse-drawn wagon. True to his upbringing, Smucker took great pride in a job well done and signed the lid of every crock of apple butter as his personal promise and guarantee of quality. By adhering to a simple set of beliefs and promises that focus on quality, people, ethics, and growth, the company leads in each of its selected retail food segments in North America, with sales of more than $2 billion annually.

Building a distinctive personal brand of living and leadership is no different. Great leaders consistently make good on a distinctive set of promises. Their value and influence are built upon the management and daily implementation of those promises. In short, they daily embody the promises of their leadership brand.

Ronald Wilson Reagan, fortieth president of the United States and one of America's greatest statesmen, is a textbook example of how a leader effectively used a compelling set of ideas to create distinctive leadership. Mr. Reagan built his brand of global leadership on the daily management and implementation of four distinct ideas. He promised that his administration would be built on these ideas:

America can do better.
Defense matters.
Communism is evil.
Big government is bad.

These four principles underpinned everything he stood for and worked to achieve during his days in the White House. He spawned optimism in the face of national malaise under the Carter Administration because he taught and promised that *America can do better.* He built a strong military, won battles, and increased morale among United States troops because he believed that *defense matters.*

In one of his presidency's most defining moments, following through on his conviction that *Communism is evil*, Mr. Reagan offered a dramatic challenge to Mikhail Gorbachev at one of the Cold War's most noted landmarks, the Brandenburg Gate that divided Berlin. In a speech to a large crowd gathered on the west side of the closed gates, Reagan emotionally and theatrically pleaded, "Mr. Gorbachev, tear down this wall!"[21]

The wall did come down and Gorbachev eventually became one of Reagan's most ardent admirers, participating in Reagan's funeral and saying his distinctive leadership flowed from his optimism and the strength of his ideas.[22] In fact, Ronald Reagan himself said the following: "to grasp and hold a vision is the very essence of leadership."[23]

Finally, his famous state of the union address expressed that *big government is bad* when he had a fleet of wheel barrows deliver volumes upon volumes of budget documents to his podium during his speech, making a mockery of the complexity of the U.S. congressional budgetary process.

An Example: The Pretty Good Student

After working with undergraduate business students at two universities for nearly twenty years, I'm very proud of the many who stand out from the crowd.

But I can also tell you that many students desire to be average or common. Most freshmen cower regarding greatness. They begin their collegiate experience attending to generic life. Their visions are shallow, myopic, and focused mainly on personal survival. Their benchmarks are set predominantly by their peers and society at large.

Few students have visions of excellence or distinction when they enter college. That is why I have dedicated my life to "higher education"—which is another way to say, "education from above" that is powered by God's perspective. I seek to create visions of excellence and produce a brand of education that is eternal. I hope and pray someday all my students see their true potential.

Each year, my first attack against the notion of generic comes at the beginning of the semester. I have my students stand in our first class together and read aloud Charles Osgood's poem entitled "Pretty Good." I read the poem aloud. Students repeat the refrain, "pretty good." Imagine the classroom scene the first day of class as a freshman.

There once was a pretty good student who sat in a pretty good class.
And he had a pretty good teacher who always let pretty good pass.
He wasn't terrific at reading. He wasn't a whiz-bang at math.
But for him, education was leading straight down a pretty good path.
He didn't find school too exciting, though he wanted to do pretty well.
He did have some trouble with writing because nobody had taught him
    to spell.
When doing arithmetic problems, pretty good was regarded as fine.
Five plus five needn't always add up to ten. A pretty good answer was nine.
The pretty good class that he sat in was there in a pretty good school.
And this student was not an exception. On the contrary, he was the rule.
The pretty good school that he went to was there in a pretty good town.
And nobody seemed to notice, he couldn't tell a verb from a noun.
This pretty good student in fact, was part of a pretty good mob.
And the first time he knew what he lacked, was when he
looked for a pretty good job. It was then, when he sought
a position, he discovered that life could be tough.
And he soon had a sneaking suspicion, pretty good
might not be good enough. The pretty good town in our story
was there in a pretty good state, which had pretty good aspirations,
and prayed for a pretty good fate. There once was a pretty good nation,
proud of the greatness it had, which learned much too late,
if you want to be great, pretty good, is in fact, pretty bad.[24]

All too often, the *pretty good* student wants opportunities to participate in the best classes, premium internships, and high-paying jobs. Unfortunately, on earth and in heaven, *pretty good* earns few opportunities and rewards. Time and again the "good enough" worker wonders why she was released from her job. Too often the "average" business finds itself in decline and financial turmoil. Ordinary church leaders discover, to their surprise, that the body is dying. Run-of-the-mill husbands and wives find their partners solemn and their marriages falling apart. Mediocre parents struggle over the moral and spiritual drift of their children. Please know that lives of distinction never result from ordinary living. Good enough never is!

Bringing It Home

Once while teaching in the marketplace, Jesus told a great story about true value. An employer gave three workers money according to their abilities. Two workers doubled their money. A third worker buried his money. When the employer asked how they were doing, he was happy that two of his workers doubled his investments. He was furious at the one who had buried the money and returned the same amount. The employer said the third worker could have at least put the money in the bank to draw interest. Then he fired the third worker, calling him a wicked, lazy servant.[25]

Burying your talent is easy. You need no desire to be great, no set of deliberate practices, and you certainly have no need for a distinctive and compelling set of promises and actions. You won't stand for anything, and no one will follow.

On the other hand, if you want to do something extraordinary with what you have been given by God, you are moving toward the starting line in the race to build a brand that matters. You can take your talents and multiply them and not only bring your employer but your Creator a great return on the investment in your life.

Remember, this path is not easy. Most defect. In the next chapter, we'll look at the top killer of a leadership brand that matters!

Key Points

1. A leadership brand is strategically built through the understanding, utilization, and management of God's 4 "P"s: Perspective, Position, Power, and Promise.
2. That which is generic has no lasting power or influence. Great brands hold great power and influence.
3. A brand is a mark that identifies ownership.
4. Great brands are built by intense desire and hard work.
5. Great brands manage and deliver a set of distinctive promises.
6. Good is the enemy of great. Ordinary is easy. Great is difficult.
7. Generic is determined by the masses. Distinctive is determined by God.

Challenge

Is good really the enemy of great? Is it really a sin to be ordinary? The answer depends on how you answer this question: Was Jesus ordinary? If you are honest, it will be difficult, at best, to say that Jesus was an ordinary individual whose teachings call you and me to common living.

Jesus' brand of leadership is like none other. His work among men left a legacy of leadership the world will never forget. His disciples were forever changed. His teachings caused people to focus on different things—mostly things unseen. The apostle Paul reasoned with individuals to focus on unseen things above and think about things that are true, noble, right, pure, lovely, admirable, excellent, or praiseworthy (Phil. 4:8). In other words, Paul admonishes us to think about eternal things! These things will lead you to greatness.

Exploring Big Ideas

1. Describe some attributes of products that have strong brand names.

2. Why are strongly branded products so powerful and influential for consumers?

3. Explain why clear purpose, desire, and hard work precede the building of great brands.

4. Do you think many people put as much effort into building Jesus' brand of living and leadership in their lives (families, churches, communities) as companies do with their brands? Why or why not?

5. Help define the difference between each of the talented people in Matthew 25. List some attributes of people you know who are developing a brand of leadership that matters.

6. What caused Moses to finally envision a brand of greatness in their lives?

7. In your opinion, why don't the masses envision greatness? Is it really a sin to be ordinary?

Chapter Two

Brand Killer Number One: The Voice of the Crowd

"What shall I do, then, with Jesus who is called Christ?"
They all answered, "Crucify him!"

—Matthew 27:22

The crowd shouts loudly when leaders lead. This competing collective voice can often trip up people you are coaching or managing. On the basketball court, it confused the girls we coached, and they were playing wildly. When I told one girl, "Keep the ball moving, work the ball around the court," people behind me in the stands shouted, "Take the ball and shoot it! Shoot it! Shoot it!" Not exactly what I had in mind!

When Jesus went before Pontius Pilate, the Roman official said, "What shall I do, then, with Jesus who is called Christ?"

They all answered, "Crucify him!"

"'Why? What crime has he committed?' Pilate asked.

But they shouted all the louder, 'Crucify him!'

When Pilate saw that he was getting nowhere, but that instead an uproad was starting, he took water and washed his hands in front of the crowd. 'I am innocent of this man's blood,' he said, 'It is your responsibility!'"[1]

Pilate made a crucial mistake in leadership. He listened to the *voice of the crowd*. He shifted the responsibility, though God gave it to him. Pilate failed to understand the significance of his position under God. Thus, he failed his mission. The voice of the crowd was powerful and Pilate was afraid to exercise his authority.

From the early formation of Israel, God valued a person speaking up for the innocent and not listening to the crowd. In Leviticus, God declares, "If a person sins because he does not speak up when he hears a public charge to testify regarding something he has *seen* [emphasis mine] or learned about, he will be held responsible."[2]

Pilate was guilty of not speaking up regarding what he knew. How about you? Do you stand tall when the crowd is attacking you?

Aaron failed, big time, to provide leadership and influence for Moses and the Lord. While Moses hiked Mt. Sinai and received the Ten Commandments, Aaron failed to understand the significance of his position, bowing to the voice of the crowd. "Do not be angry, my lord," Aaron answered. "You know how prone these people are to evil. They said to me, 'Make us gods who will go before us. As for this fellow Moses who brought us up out of Egypt, we don't know what has happened to him.' So I told them, 'Whoever has any gold jewelry, take it off.' Then they gave me the gold, and I threw it into the fire, and out came this calf!"[3]

A calf just jumped out of the fire? No, but the calf did come to exist because Aaron listened to the voice of the crowd and failed to make a call for righteousness. Therefore, confusion reigned. "Moses saw that the people were running wild and that Aaron had let them get out of control and so they became laughing stock to their enemies."[4]

The voice of the crowd presents a temptation as common and old as the world itself. The story of Adam, Eve, and the serpent presents an excellent, yet lamentable, illustration:

> Now the serpent was more crafty than any of the wild animals the Lord
> God had made. He said to the woman, "Did God really say, 'You must
> not eat from any tree in the garden'?" Eve said . . . God did say, 'You
> must not eat fruit from the tree that is in the middle of the garden, and
> you must not touch it, or you will surely die.'"
> "You will not surely die," the serpent said to the woman.[5]

God had given Adam and Eve an important position in the garden for a reason. They were told to take care of the earth, but they listened to the serpent instead.

Academicians use the term "social proof" to describe the voice of the crowd. This voice resonates when people find themselves in uncertain situations, looking to others for appropriate behavior. For example, a driver may be stopped at an intersection where the traffic light seems to be unusually long in changing. Most drivers begin to sense that the light should have already changed to green. However, the bright red signal serves as a deterrent to law-abiding and safety-conscious drivers. The driver looks around to see what others are doing. Each vehicle remains stopped at the light. But, sure enough, one driver decides to proceed through the intersection. What happens? Everyone follows. This socially constructed phenomenon is called social proof, a decision-making mechanism people use when faced with uncertain situations.

Most of us conform to the crowd on a daily basis. Your clothing, style of hair, house, and job are all, in part, based on what is socially acceptable. As you read this, you might deny that you engage in such petty behavior! Let me offer a challenge. Take an old family picture, school picture, or picture with some of your contemporaries from at least fifteen years ago. As you examine the picture, would you say you look more similar or dissimilar to those with whom you are photographed? Chances are you look quite similar to those with you in the picture. Your hair is probably similar in style to your friends. You are probably dressed in similar clothing that reflects the trends of the day. If you are in front of a car, it displays the unique styling and design features of that generation's automobiles. These evidences of social proof exist because our choices are socially constructed. In other words, we tend to live, consume, and behave mostly the way others do and we often do so because of what other people think.

Dennis the Menace, Mr. Wilson, and Fashion

In an old *Dennis the Menace* television program, Mr. Wilson gathers a group of his friends together after dinner in his backyard to watch him using his new telescope. Each of the men is about forty years old, dressed in dark, narrow lapel suits, white shirts, and skinny ties. Two of them wear hats, two of them are smoking pipes, and all of them have short greased-back hair. The attire of these men is quite appropriate for the early 1950s.

However, if one of my forty-something friends showed up at my house after dinner today wearing a dark suit, white shirt, skinny tie, hat, and smoking a pipe, I would be amused. Why? Because these "manly" fashion items are not in sync with today's styles. What is fashion? It's what other people say looks good and appropriate.

As a college professor, I continue to stand in amazement at the types and styles of clothing that come into my classroom. If I ever wore an earring when I was in college, I would have faced collegial harassment. If I wore sagging-off-your-hip pants, I would have been laughed off campus. In fact, I probably would have received a phone call from the dean's office. If my shorts hung down past my knees when I played basketball, people would have offered safety pins to help. All students dress to some level of conformity, depending on their campus and what students on their campus say is socially acceptable.

We must understand one simple truth. The voice of the crowd only matters if the "crowd" matters to you. If you don't care what the crowd thinks, then you are not likely to comply or conform to its desires. If the crowd is important to you, however, you face an immediate and powerful leadership brand killer. Pilate longed for the acceptance of the crowd. He knew they could take his position in society if word got back to Rome about how he allowed a civil uproar. In the end, his brand died.

Social Drinking and Conformity

I remember watching an episode of *20/20* in which John Stoessel went undercover to explore the social nature of college drinking. He solicited two groups, twenty college students in each, to participate in his study. All of the students were from Penn State University, long known as a nationally ranked "party school." His request was to observe them on film during parties that would be given for them on Friday and Saturday nights. They agreed. His camera crews geared up and the partying began.

The first group was filmed on Friday night. It was a lively group. Stoessel held the party at a bar. As the evening passed, students became more and more intoxicated. Their behavior slid off the table. A group of males entered into a beer-chugging contest. One young man vomited. The alcohol was clearly causing them to lose control. The evening ended, and the students were escorted home.

On Saturday evening, the second group was filmed. It was also a lively group. The party was held at the same location. The behavior of the second group mirrored that of the first. As the evening passed, student behavior became less controlled and clearly impacted by the consumption of alcohol served at the party. Another group of young men engaged in a beer-chugging contest. Another young man vomited. The evening ended, and the students were escorted home.

Sunday was a day of recovery. On Monday evening, Stoessel conducted a live television broadcast and interview with the students as they watched themselves on film from the parties on Friday and Saturday. He questioned them about their behavior. Some could not remember. At one point during the interview, Stoessel turned toward the group that was filmed on Saturday. The cameras closed in and focused on their faces. He explained to them that not one drop of alcohol had been served at their party. As he allowed them to watch themselves one more time on film, profound physiological signs of guilt and embarrassment swept over their bodies and faces. Their behavior exactly paralleled that of the Friday night group where alcohol was served! They were behaving as they "thought" they should behave to conform to the desires of the crowd in that particular situation. It was social proof, pure and simple.[6]

A Birthday Party at McDonalds

In one of my consumer behavior classes at Abilene Christian University, I share the results from a variety of studies on social proof and conformance. There are many fascinating studies to learn from. I typically share John Stoessel's study because it is interesting and provocative. Once, after I shared the results of the study, a young man said that he and a group of friends had recently thrown a birthday party for a friend at McDonalds.

Evidently, they had purchased a variety of helium-filled balloons to use at the party. At one point, they passed a helium-filled balloon around the circle. Each person inhaled and spoke in their resulting high-pitched voices. As the balloon passed to the birthday girl, it was switched for a normal balloon filled with carbon dioxide. Unaware of the switch, she inhaled and began to speak in a high-pitched voice for the crowd. I felt sorry for the girl when I heard the story, but it did highlight my point quite well.

A Harvard University Experience

During the summer of 2002, I attended a summer institute for Management and Leadership Education at Harvard University. The class was extremely valuable to my own personal and professional growth and development. It was well planned and executed. The content was solid. The teachers were excellent. They provided some of the best teaching I have ever experienced. Among the many things I observed during the two-week course was what I would call the emptiness of the crowd. Its voice was impotent, without hope.

Important issues in higher education were discussed throughout this course. There was, however, a surprising underlying theme in the course content: spirituality in our roles as leaders. All eighty-five participants were provosts, deans, and/or directors from institutions of higher learning across the United States and thirteen foreign nation states. Class members represented schools like Aalborg University (Denmark), Abilene Christian University, the University of Southern California, Harvard University, the Pennsylvania State University, Belmont University, the University of Massachusetts, the University of Texas, Pepperdine University, the University of Hong Kong, Loughborough University (United Kingdom), and the University of Calgary.

It was broadly agreed that spirituality was central to the work of leadership in higher education. Issues of life, meaning, and purpose reside in this realm and it is important to the work of higher education, spoke the participants. All agreed that, as leaders, we needed to be spiritual people paying attention to spiritual things. One dean said that within this spiritual realm, truth is to be found.

From these conversations, student life professionals in our class contemplated and discussed spirituality and their new uncertainty regarding university students since the terrible acts of September 11, 2001. Dr. Peggy Patterson, dean of student life at the University of Calgary, noted that illnesses reported at the Health Services Clinic had risen dramatically during the year after 9/11. Demand for counseling services had increased, but also demand for physical health services had increased to before-unseen levels. Outbreaks of meningitis, autoimmune diseases, and flu increased dramatically. "Immune systems are being pushed beyond normal limits due to unanswered questions and the resulting stress that these unanswered questions cause," Dr. Patterson said.

Interestingly, the conversation ended in some level of despair because professors had no real answers to these conditions. They simply offered impassioned prose that sought to point their students to the realm of the "spirit." Spirituality was never defined nor addressed with substance. It was referred to vaguely as "joy," "spirit," "soul," "force," and "love" throughout the course. In the end, the tough questions of life, meaning, purpose, and death were left unaddressed.

Throughout the course, class members shared intimate stories of personal struggle for meaning. One of our classmates experienced the drug-related death of his nephew during the week. He and I had an opportunity to visit one day as we rode on a bus to Boston Harbor, and I conveyed my sorrow for the death of his nephew. He said that his nephew's death was tragic. I agreed. He stated that his philosophy of life and death could be summarized as qué será, será (whatever will be, will be). I explained that I believed in God and heaven. He was quiet. I explained that I pray to God daily. I pray that my wife, my children, and I will make good choices and lead significant lives. He asked what I got for "all that praying." I suggested true life and meaning.

At the end of one of our sessions on leadership, we were discussing a book written by Terrence Deal and Lee Bolman entitled *Leading with Soul*.[7] The premise of the book is that the search for soul and spirit, for depth and meaning in our lives, is fueling a powerful and growing twenty-first-century leadership movement. As Dr. Bolman led us down a long path bordered with spiritual landscaping, he explained how interesting and beautiful the spirit is in our lives. Unfortunately, he ended the journey with these hopeless lines from the thirteenth-century poet, Rumi:

> All day I think about it, then at night I say it.
> Where did I come from,
> and what am I supposed to be doing?
> I have no idea.
> My soul is from elsewhere, I'm sure of that,
> and I intend to end up there.

Oh, the confusion and sadness in the room! At Harvard, the nation's first university, founded in 1636 on the premise that God was central to higher education, educators left the auditorium somber and silent. The voice of the crowd had nothing to offer.

In my mind, Jesus softly spoke, "You diligently study the Scriptures because you think that by them you possess eternal life. These are the Scriptures that testify about me, yet you refuse to come to me to have life."[8] Joining the discussion is the apostle Peter as he speaks eloquently to empty life and contrasts it with life in the Spirit:

> For you know that it was not with perishable things such as silver or
> gold that you were redeemed from the empty way of life handed down
> to you from your forefathers, but with the precious blood of Christ, a

lamb without blemish or defect. He was chosen before the creation of
the world, but was revealed in these last times for your sake. Through
him you believe in God, who raised him from the dead and glorified
him, and so your faith and hope are in God . . . and the one who trusts
in him will never be put to shame.[9]

Because we all have competing voices, even when reading, I want to reiterate a
few points. First, the voice of the crowd is real. Second, it is powerful but ultimately empty. Third, when heard over the voice of God, it prevents individuals,
families, churches, businesses, cities, states, and nations from building a brand
that matters! The voice of the crowd builds no distinction! All under its watch
and influence remain ordinary. Too often, it causes people to transfer the responsibility of leadership and aborts our God-given missions.

A Harsh Rebuke

The Lord strongly rebukes those who conform to the voice of the crowd. He says,
"How can you believe if you accept praise from one another, yet make no effort
to obtain the praise that comes from the only God?"[10] In fact, the power of the
crowd's voice is so significant, Jesus said the Jews "could not" believe because
they loved the praises of men more than praise from God.[11] The apostle Paul was
strong on this point, as well. That is why he said, "Do not conform any longer to
the pattern of this world, but be transformed by the renewing of your mind."[12]

Be mindful that the voice of the crowd presses toward a generic brand of
leadership, but the voice of God builds a brand of leadership with power to
change what really matters!

Key Points

1. The voice of the crowd is real.
2. The voice of the crowd is powerful!
3. The voice of the crowd prevents leaders from taking charge when put in charge.
4. Everyone gives in to the voice of the crowd at some level.
5. The voice of the crowd only matters if the crowd matters to you.
6. Jesus often harshly rebukes the crowds for their propensity to conform.
7. According to Jesus, you cannot believe if you love the praises of men more than the praises of God.

Challenge

Crucify Him! Crucify Him! The voice of the crowd rings eternally in our ears. Pilate gives in. He loses the battle. Why? Because he was afraid of the crowd and wanted to save his own skin. His decision prevented him from believing.

Imagine an official on a basketball court who can hear the crowds screaming. There are many perspectives. Traveling, double-dribble, out-of-bounds, foul! These are too tough to call. The official gives in. He makes no calls. He fails to see the significance of his position, so he misses his appointment with destiny.

Jesus said clearly, if anyone loves the praises of men more than the praises of God, they will be prevented from belief (John 5:44). I have enough difficulty believing and staying on track. The last thing I need is more to hold me back!

Exploring Big Ideas

1. Why is the voice of the crowd so overwhelming at times?

2. Describe a time in your life when you gave in to the crowd.

3. Describe a time in your life when you were able to stand up and be counted.

4. Why are some people able to withstand the crowd when others are not?

5. What can be done to produce change in the crowd?

6. Really, why did Pilate give in? What must have been running through his mind at the time?

7. Does the voice of the crowd matter to you? If so, why? If not, why not?

Chapter Three

BRAND KILLER NUMBER TWO: THE OPPONENT

Put on the full armor of God so that you can take your stand
against the devil's schemes. For our struggle is not
against flesh and blood . . .

—EPHESIANS 6:11-12

Behind the voice of the crowd is a real killer. He is focused and tenacious. He is authentic: the father of lies. He goes by Satan, Lucifer, anti-Christ, serpent, deceiver. He is evil personified, and his power is out of this world. In many arenas, he is the victor, winning mightily. His work is most often subtle, seductive, and destructive. The following story illustrates his work.

Eskimo wolf hunters use a simple, ancient technique to trap and kill wolves. The Eskimo hunter sharpens his knife, dips it in animal blood and freezes it. In a continuous iterative process, the hunter dips the knife in blood, freezes it, dips it in blood, and freezes it. He repeats the process until the knife looks like a frozen popsicle. The knife is then put out in the snow. Soon, a wolf begins to lick the frozen blood. It keeps licking until, eventually, the frozen blood numbs the wolf's tongue and it doesn't notice the knife beginning to cut. Without realizing, the wolf continues to lick until it dies—strangled in its own blood.

Satan's work often looks like a frozen popsicle. People often engage the popsicle, enjoying the pleasure of the first few licks. But, after some time, the subtle addictive nature of the popsicle results in a slow, bloody death. Through a new "acceptable" level of evil allowed to permeate our lives today, we find ourselves ever more numbed to the knife of Satan, the killer.

A majority of people today believe Satan simply to be symbolic of that which some might consider "evil." Recent work by the Barna Group suggests that only twenty-eight percent of Christian adolescents in the United States believe Satan to be real. Furthermore, their findings reveal that seven out of ten Christian adolescents believe all people experience the same post-death experience regardless of their beliefs. Amazing![1]

In his famous book, *The Screwtape Letters*, C. S. Lewis describes the deception of Satan's earthly work. Uncle Screwtape teaches Wormwood, "Thanks to the processes which we [devils] set at work in them [man] centuries ago, they find it all but impossible to believe in the unfamiliar while the familiar is before their eyes. Keep pressing home on him [man] the *ordinariness* of things."[2] Moreover,

> "My dear Wormwood, I wonder you should ask me whether it is essential to keep the patient [humans] in ignorance of your own existence [devils]. That question, at least for the present phase of the struggle, has been answered for us by the High Command [Satan]. Our policy for the moment is to conceal ourselves. . . . I do not think you will have much difficulty in keeping the patient [man] in the dark. The fact that 'devils' are predominantly *comic* figures in the modern imagination will help you. If any faint suspicion of your existence begins to arise in his mind [man], suggest to him a picture of something in red tights, and persuade him that since he cannot believe in that (it is an old textbook method of confusing them) he therefore cannot believe in you."[3]

Satan's *ordinary* work came a bit too close to home several years back while my family and I were on sabbatical near the University of Michigan. Michelle, a fifth grader at the time, was with me one day as I stood on the high school campus near the front doors waiting to pick up Kelly, a freshman, after school. Mobs of students poured out of the building and whirled past us as they made their way to the parking lots to go home for the day. Finally, Kelly came out to meet us. As we hugged and got ready to head home, we heard shouting break out between two boys nearby. At the top of their lungs, they shouted obscenities back and forth while clutching their girlfriends like pawns. They were dropping the "F" bomb, as my children would say. It was evil, vicious, and frightening.

Everyone was laughing. I was shocked! I yelled out, "Hey, watch your language." The mob was stunned when they heard this mid-lifer telling them to knock it off. They looked at me and then at one another. I thought a fight might break out. After a brief moment of hesitation, they stopped. In retaliation, a few weeks later as Kelly walked to basketball practice, two guys yelled out to her, "Hey, can you do some porno tricks for us?" She turned and said, "You are sick!" Agreed. Satan is not healthy. The next day, several girls warned Kelly to beware of the "freshmeat" syndrome. They explained that many guys in the high school like to grope the bottoms and breasts of new freshmen girls. Again, sickening. Satan cheapens life through the destruction of others.

Satan is not some existential force or philosophical idea, though his work is often disguised and un-discerned. In reality, his accomplishments are very impressive. Examine some of his statistics against the American family:

1. Today, in the U.S. alone, there are nineteen million new cases of sexually transmitted infections reported each year. Half of these cases occur among 15–24 year-olds.[4]

2. The Centers for Disease Control and Prevention recently released a study indicating that 1 in 4 teen girls, or 3.2 million, are infected with a sexually transmitted infection.[5]

3. Over fifty percent of teens will use drugs, fifteen percent will become addicted, and others will die from drug overuse.[6]

4. According to a survey of thirty thousand teens released by the National Campaign to Prevent Teen Pregnancy, twenty percent of teens lose their virginity before their fifteenth birthday. By the time teens graduate high school, two-thirds have had intercourse, and when they walk down the aisle, a mere fifteen percent will still be virgins.[7]

5. About one in three women will have an abortion by age forty-five. Additionally, fifty percent of U.S. women having abortions are younger than twenty-five years old.[8]

6. The U.S. Supreme Court overturned anti-sodomy laws that were on the books in thirteen states, overturning their own 1986 ruling on the subject.[9]

7. According to a 2003 U.S. Census Bureau report, 2.4 million grandparents are raising their grandchildren as the primary

caregivers, often because their own sons and daughters are in jail or on drugs and alcohol.[10]

8. America continues to have the highest divorce rate of any industrialized nation. Forty to fifty percent of marriages end in divorce. Sixty percent of re-marriages end in divorce.[11]

9. Over four million women are abused annually in their homes. This translates into one woman being abused every fifteen seconds.[12]

10. Approximately four to ten million children annually witness their mother's abuse.[13]

11. Approximately four out of ten children do not live with their biological fathers.[14]

12. Approximately three out of ten children live in a home without a father of any kind.[15]

13. Approximately fifty to seventy percent of singles co-habitat outside of marriage. This segment is the largest and fastest growing segment in American society.[16]

Against American culture during the last decade, some of Satan's statistics look like this:

1. Beginning spring season 2010, television viewers began to see full-frontal male nudity, graphic sexual activity (heterosexual, homosexual, and group), and explicit violence that had rarely if ever previously seen on mainstream TV.[17]

2. International Planned Parenthood Foundation's recently released report, "Stand and Deliver: Sex, Health and Young People in the 21st Century," promotes contraceptive sex education for children as young as ten years old.[18]

3. Public Law 103-160—which declares that the "presence in the armed forces of persons who demonstrate a propensity or intent to engage in homosexual acts would create an unacceptable risk to the high standards of morale, good order and discipline, and unit cohesion that are the essence of military capability"—is currently under attack (2010), and many seek its reversal.[19]

4. The Obama administration is requiring military bases worldwide to carry Levonorgestrel, or "Plan B," a drug that prevents a fertilized embryo from implanting in the uterus and thereby destroys a human life.[20]

5. In 2001, a public library in Boulder, Colorado, featured an art exhibit comprised of twenty-one ceramic penises strung on a closeline that ended in a noose, under the title "Hanging 'Em Out to Dry."[21]

6. A recent study indicates that among young adults (18–29), sixty-one percent say that same-sex marriages should be valid.[22]

7. San Francisco officials voted 9–2 to make their city the first in the nation to pay for sex-change operations for city employees. The cost to taxpayers will be considerable. The increase in premiums will mean an estimated $683,000 in new city labor costs.[23]

8. The Episcopal Church approved its first openly gay bishop on August 5, 2003, hours after he was cleared of a variety of misconduct allegations.[24]

9. The Episcopal Church gave official recognition to same-sex unions on August 7, 2003, two days after ratifying the church's first openly gay bishop.[25]

10. President Obama's education czar, Kevin Jennings, founder of the Gay, Lesbian, and Straight Education Network (GLSEN), has spoken and written of his counseling a 15-year-old male student who engaged in homosexual acts with an older man in a bus station bathroom. Rather than report the statutory rape as required by state law, Jennings merely encouraged the boy to use a condom in such encounters.[26]

11. In March 2009, one-time Nasdaq chairman Bernard Madoff pled guilty to operating a fifty billion dollar Ponzi scheme—the largest in known history—paying off early investors with funds from subsequent clients to keep the illusion of profit alive.[27]

Personal Observations—Confusion and Hurt

As an educator on a Christian university campus, I daily witness confusion and hurt in students' lives. These young people struggle with sin, relativism, promiscuity, and moral apathy regarding eternal purposes just like the rest of us. I continue to see Satan's pervasive, devastating, and debilitating idea of divorce affecting the lives of students on our campus. Students are struggling with life, the Lord, and their own beliefs and feelings about marriage. They hurt inside as they realize that their personal sense of security and self-worth has been challenged by the actions of their parents. It is hard for many to believe that married couples can stay committed, in love, and together for a lifetime under God. It is extremely difficult for them to develop a vision of marital commitment and purity when they have not seen it themselves.

Most recently, I witnessed a marriage being destroyed after only fifteen months. The reason: internet pornography. Hurt, pain, bitterness, sin, hatred, jealousy—they were all present. The young man told me he knew that once the divorce was finished, things "would work out for the glory of God." He explained that God had other plans for him. He was thankful that they didn't have any children. It was as if his marriage had just been a little playtime and now he could start all over again and really glorify God. It was disturbing and heartbreaking. He was licking the popsicle!

Reality check! Satan is alive and there is much confusion in our world. People are running wild. They are outside the boundaries. They are being hurt. They are hurting themselves. They are hurting others, tripping and falling down. Lives are being destroyed.

Public vs. Private

Beyond what I have just described, what causes me great alarm is the isolationism that exists with many Christians. I sense, particularly in our Christian college population, a growing sense of apathy and disinterest toward the problems noted. Their actions seem to say, "no big deal." These issues are a given for everyone. This apathetic orientation toward making a difference in the daily world of business, commerce, and government prevails with many.

Those who are deeply committed to Christ often would rather do youth ministry at a local church than be involved in the broader struggle in the global marketplace. Please don't misquote me. I want the best and the brightest among us to work with our children in our churches. However, if none of us is willing to take a stand in the marketplace, it is over. Leadership that matters cannot exist in isolation!

It seems to me that the broader Christian community participates fully in our culture from a secular perspective. We work. We play. We go to school. We consume. We enjoy leisure activities and entertainment. However, we are not actively leading people in most of these areas of our lives. Our leadership energies are reserved for the "work of the church" on Sundays and Wednesdays. Therefore, the model for many Christians is to blend with society but have great "praise and worship" on Sundays. In essence, we have constructed a paradigm that says it is appropriate to keep our religion private. Thus, as a people, we tend to be "of the world but not in it" instead of "in the world but not of it."

It parallels the development of the constitutional law of religion that has gone from public to private in the United States over the last sixty years. From the founding era at the end of the eighteenth century until well into the twentieth century, Christian religion was thought to be a significant and legitimate component of American public life. By the 1940s, however, American public life had become largely secular, although large numbers of Americans remained committed to traditional religious beliefs and practices in their private lives. The American Court's struggle has been one of defining the appropriate relationship between religion and government within the context of a secular public that considers religion a predominantly private activity of no unique social significance.[28]

I can assure you that the opponent is quite happy with our private "praise and worship" because it doesn't impact anyone on his team. Our efforts and labors often have no impact on our culture. If the world were a fifteen thousand square foot home, the church would spend most of its time in the second-floor game room. It would have a nice time "praising and worshiping" but would never impact the rest of the people and activities in the house.

When I first walked on the campus of Abilene Christian University two decades ago, I quickly found out that business students sometimes felt ashamed of their major. They believed it was more noble or sacred to be a Bible major. They were afraid of engaging the culture as a business person. Comfort for them was found in the confines of the work of the local church.

As a newly minted Ph.D. and business professor, I objected! I still object! The call to be a Bible major is not more holy than that of a business major or premed major or education major. In fact, I personally believe that viewpoint to be significantly skewed. Again, please don't get me wrong. We need the best and the brightest among us to be involved in teaching and preaching the gospel and equipping the saints for ministry. However, not all people go to church but nearly everybody goes to work! If we are all in the church building, who is going to be on the streets, in the office, in the schools, and in the hospitals, helping with the mass confusion and pain that exists? Who will provide strong moral leadership in our businesses, our communities, our school systems, and our homes? The answer comes from the lips of Jesus, "You did not choose me, I chose you to go and bear fruit—fruit that will last."[29] This is no ordinary fruit, growing only in orchards where distinctive leadership matters!

In the next section, we will continue our leadership work by examining our second "P," Position. Distinctive leaders take charge of their current positions in life and make them the focus of their earthly work. Let's take a look.

Key Points

1. The opponent is real and formidable. He is not some existential force or philosophical idea. His work is best described as a "roaring lion seeking whom he may devour."[30]
2. The opponent has a well-crafted game plan and an eternal appetite for winning.
3. The opponent rules the world and works in those who are disobedient.[31]
4. The more Satan can keep the faith of Christians private, the broader and stronger his domain of influence.
5. Satan often implements his game plan through the voice of the crowd!
6. The opponent's work has significantly and negatively impacted the world as we know it today.
7. Satan is the master of deception.

Challenge

These words, like those of a weak basketball official, at first may seem reasonable—"just let 'em play." It doesn't really matter anyway. Who said it was your responsibility to provide leadership, direction, help, and healing on the court? Someone else will come along after the game and deal with the carnage. Perhaps it is just not your job.

It is your job! The opponent is real. He is formidable. He is a seller of *ideas* distributed through the voice of the crowd. His *ideas* are engineered and manufactured for mass distribution. They corrupt good soil, filling it with weeds that choke and destroy good things (Matt. 13:39). He has schemes and sets traps (Eph. 6:11, 1 Tim. 3:7). He is a tempter (Matt. 4:1). He seeks authority and power (Matt 4:5–8). He is a roaring lion seeking whom he may devour (I Pet. 5:7–8).

Why don't we talk about him anymore? It seems he is rarely mentioned in our churches. His name is rarely found on our lips. Is it a bit too silly for us to believe the devil is real? After all, we are in the twenty-first century. We are a sophisticated people. We have gone to the moon. Our enemies can be targeted and destroyed with precision-guided missiles. Our digital technology promises unprecedented accomplishment. Perhaps Satan is simply an *idea* whose time has come and gone. God forbid! Evidence of his damage is all around us. His work is no less passionate and targeted today than it was in the Garden of Eden thousands of years ago. His mission is clear: lead people away from Jesus.

One of the main reasons Jesus was sent to earth was to destroy his work (1 John 3:8). Maybe we should be a bit more contemplative about the parallel reason for our lives on earth. It just sounds wrong, doesn't it? It seems too radical and uneducated for today's modern society. In fact, if we talk about the devil, others may be turned off. As I write this, I am remembering John the Baptist's introductory remarks in one of his first sermons. It went something like this, "You brood of vipers! Who warned you to flee from the coming wrath?" (Matt. 3:7). That will warm your audience in a big way! John's leadership was extremely distinctive. He called it like he saw it. Maybe we should consider the opponent again.

Exploring Big Ideas

1. Do you think people, in general, really believe there is an opponent? Why? Why not?

2. Why does Satan go unnoticed all the time? Is evil more difficult to comprehend than good?

3. Explain your perspective of what happened in the Garden of Eden (Genesis 3). How did Satan accomplish his mission in the garden?

4. How did Jesus withstand the power of the opponent (Luke 4:1–13)?

5. Why don't we hear lessons or sermons about Satan?

6. Do you think hell is real?

7. Why do you think so many believe Satan's offers are so good?

Part Two

POSITION

Chapter Four

WHEN IN CHARGE, TAKE CHARGE

There are two types of people
who never achieve very much in their lifetimes.
One is the person who won't do what he is told to do,
and the other is the person who does no more than he is told to do.

—ANDREW CARNEGIE

Four-star Army General Wayne Downing, at one time, had command over all U.S. Special Forces worldwide. As a noted global military leader and strategist, he was called out of retirement to consult with President George W. Bush on the eve of September 11, 2001, and he was often called to serve as a special military analyst for NBC News.

I've had the honor of knowing General Downing personally, and during lunch one day, he told me his number one motto for leadership is this:

"When in charge, take charge."

Positions, he said, are given for a reason. They are given to accomplish specific missions. When people abdicate the responsibility embedded in their given positions, they render the position and the mission unachievable. In short, he said, if you have been put in charge, take charge!

The Purpose Driven Life by Rick Warren has led millions of people worldwide to understand and live out their purpose. Much has been said in many books and sermons about purpose, but little has been said and taken to heart about position. As Warren states in his book, "It's not about you." It's about what you do with what you have been given. We don't rise to positions on our own. We are put there for a reason. Understanding how we're put there and how to take charge once we are put there is the subject of this chapter.

"If you see a turtle on a fencepost, you know one thing for certain," says Mark Twain. "Someone put him there!" ("Or," as a good ol' Texan told me one time, "there could have been a flood!") Like the turtle, we did not arrive in our current positions by our own merit. God did it! We have been chosen by God to be "Christ's ambassadors, as though God were making his appeal through us."[1] We have been placed on the fence post of positional leadership for his glory.

Jesus understood and taught about the significance of position, as well. He explained how God "granted him authority and power over all people,"[2] such an awesome position that Paul would later say that "God gave him the name that is above every name, that at the name of Jesus every knee shall bow and every tongue confess that Jesus Christ is Lord to the glory of God the father."[3]

Jesus clearly understood the importance of his position. He understood the authority of his father in heaven. But he also knew who he was, what his position was, what his job was, and where he was going.[4] As he prayed to God about his position, he said, "For you granted him [Jesus] authority and power over all people that he might give eternal life to all those you have given him."[5] The full import of that idea is that Jesus knew that he had come from God and was returning to God.

In other venues, Jesus taught it this way:

1. **The faithful will have increased position and power.** To those who added value through the positions they had been given, he said, "Well done, good and faithful servant! You have been faithful with a few things; I will put you in charge of many things. Come and share in your master's happiness!"[6]

2. **Abusers of power will be overturned**. When some abused and perverted their given positions, Jesus reprimanded them. Once, he "overturned the tables of the money-changers and the benches

of those selling doves" because they took advantage of the people in the temple.[7]

3. **Position is linked with faith.** The Roman centurion said, "'Lord, I do not deserve to have you come under my roof. But just say the word, and my servant will be healed. For I myself am a man under authority, with soldiers under me. I tell this one, 'Go,' and he goes; and that one, 'Come,' and he comes. I say to my servant, 'Do this,' and he does it.' When Jesus heard this, he was astonished and said to those following him, 'I tell you the truth, I have not found anyone in Israel with such great faith.'"[8]

Throughout history, God has placed a high value on "take charge" people, made them his own, putting them to work. These individuals are good at what they do and use their positions in significant ways to get the job done.

How does all this connect in your life? Look at it this way. God choose faithful people to build a brand that matters. For example, Saul was good at what he did. He zealously persecuted the church, killing scores of Christians. God took Saul's talent, changed his passion with a very different "brand"—the branding iron of heaven, and then used him to lead the early church in a time of great persecution. When Saul was in charge, he took charge, and the early church was in good hands.

A different point of view reveals Jesus' perspective on the wickedness of position management failure. For example, on his way back to the city after having driven the money changers out of the temple, he cursed a fig tree by the side of the road because it failed to add value for him. He was hungry. The tree did not produce fruit. Jesus cursed it. It withered and died.[9] Unfortunately for the tree, it received the due penalty from Jesus for its lack of production. In essence, the tree used its given position for nothing.

Jesus taught this perspective through his famous parable of the talents. In the end, the person who was afraid, doing nothing with what he was given, was the one who was called a "wicked, lazy servant"![10]

As I contemplate Jesus' teaching in the context of my own life, it seems that great discouragement often results for individuals who do nothing with their positions in life. When an individual fails to take charge with a given position, power is abused. It is an abuse of power of a different kind—a failure to get the job done. Power given. No action. Power abused! Some may liken it to the stereotypical lack of responsiveness seen by the federal government during disaster relief efforts like those surrounding hurricane Katrina in 2005. If those who are put in charge fail to take charge, they abuse their positional power and people eventually suffer. It seems the Haitian relief efforts of 2010 have fared much better.

Numerous popular articles and books speak against the benefits of position. They speak of fluid, horizontal, virtual, no-cubicle, no-hierarchical workforces without boundaries. In stark contrast, Peter Drucker, perhaps the most prolific management scholar of the twentieth century, explains, "This is blatant nonsense. In any situation there has to be a final authority, that is, a 'boss'—someone who can make the final decisions and who can expect them to be obeyed."[11] In other words, someone has to be in a position to say the "buck stops here." According to Drucker, positions matter, and the way in which positions are handled matter.

People are to create value based upon the inherent obligation and potential opportunity within their positions. When obligation and opportunity meet, value and influence are created.

Power

Positions inherently come with power. If this were not the case, the intersection of obligation and opportunity would only result in frustration. As it is, power naturally results from one's position relative to others in a given social setting or social structure. Positional power is typically affiliated with a particular "office" or "function" or "responsibility." For example, if the president of the United States contacted you at home and invited you and your family to dine with him at the White House next week, most likely you would comply with his request regardless of how you cast your last ballot. You would do so because of the power of the position of president of the United States of America. This power can be used or abused, but it must be understood: it exists to create value!

Unfortunately, too many individuals fail to see the significance of their positions in life and squander value creating opportunities inherent in their given positions. Over the last two decades, in the American marketplace, we witnessed a variety of leaders who failed to understand the significance of their positions. World-class organizations like Arthur Andersen, Enron, MCI, Merrill Lynch,

Morgan Stanley, Tyco, Wachovia, Wells Fargo, and WorldCom failed. Fortunes were lost, burdensome corporate legislation was created (Sarbanes-Oxley), and lives were destroyed because leaders abdicated their fundamental responsibility to be in control and make sure the mission was being accomplished. As foreshadowed earlier, the pervasiveness of this truth came home to me a few years ago in a crowded gymnasium, on an old wooden basketball court, in West Texas.

The YMCA Basketball Court

It was an early Saturday morning in December. The *big* game was upon us! Our daughter, Hannah, seven years old at the time, would take to the court in a matter of hours and engage in her first competitive athletic event: a YMCA basketball game. As breakfast concluded, she began to "suit up." As both her father and her coach, I was feeling somewhat like I did just before she entered the world, a little anxious about the event's outcome.

I wondered if this would be a good experience for her. I wondered if this would be a good experience for me. How would she do? Would she score? Would she be a team player? Would she shoot the final shot at the buzzer for victory? How might she take the sting of defeat? Would she get hurt? Would she enjoy the game? Would we win? What lessons would she learn from this season?

In time, each of these questions was answered. I gained insight into the game of girl's youth basketball played on a varnished, stale-smelling, worn wooden court. But, more importantly, I gained insight into the game of life that is played with eternal beings on the tarnished and well-walked court we call life.

At 10:15 a.m. the teams arrived, pre-game drills were executed, the crowd grew, and finally it was time to start. We gathered our team up, said a prayer, and had a motivational "yell." Then, we sent our starting line-up out onto the floor. My daughter was looking good. The team looked great. The referee walked to the center of the court and waited. He assumed the girls would "circle up" and position themselves for the "jump ball." Unfortunately, none of our players remembered what to do (which had a lot to do with poor coaching on my part). Finally, after much confusion, the referee unable to gain control, just gave the ball to one of the girls—on the other team!

Once play began, the girls on our team seemed to have no idea where to go or what to do. Apparently the presence of an opponent caused them to fall into deep confusion. During practice we had not encountered this phenomenon.

Though they weren't perfect in practice, they always seemed to understand which basket they were to shoot for. They knew to protect the ball and keep it away from the other team. Interestingly, when encountering true opposition, our girls seemed to freeze. This was a new experience. It was a bit frightening for some. One of our players was so compliant that during the game, she simply gave the ball to a little girl on the other team who was trying to take it away! Polite, but not what we had in mind!

Second, as we discussed in chapter two, the noise from the crowd was loud and distracting. As coaches, we had not expected crowd noise to be a problem. However, our girls were constantly looking to the sidelines because they heard voices. Parents were screaming and telling their "babies" what to do. Brothers and sisters were yelling and motioning. The players were confused by all the commotion. The deafening crowd provided a variety of conflicting perspectives.

As coaches, we were unable to get the attention of our girls. They were not sensitive to our voices. Our voices didn't seem to penetrate the chatter of the crowd as it wafted across the court. We were shouting and motioning uncontrollably. The girls would turn and listen, but not to us. We were shocked. These were our team members. Why wouldn't they listen? We had worked with them, coached them, loved them, and encouraged them all during pre-season.

Then it happened. The other team began to get physical with our girls, delivering hand slaps, cross-body blocks, and swinging elbows.

"Foul!" we cried.

From the sidelines, we continuously signaled for the referee to blow a whistle. The girls were running wild and the ball was going out of bounds. The referee never blew a whistle. He simply allowed them to play it off the floor, the wall, and even the stands.

In just a matter of minutes there was total confusion on the court. The referee would not blow the whistle. He did not use his position to intervene. The ball bounced off the vinyl divider. No call. The ball bounced off the back wall. No whistle. Our girls were being hacked and hurt. Still, no call!

"That's it," I mumbled and motioned for a time out. Approaching the referee, I began to grab his whistle indicating he should consider its use. He blew the whistle. We had a talk. He explained that he was told to "let the girls play." I explained that if he continued to "let the girls play," we would see carnage on the court.

Why didn't the referee take control? I wondered. He was put in charge. Why didn't he take charge? Why didn't he execute a proper start to the game according to the rulebook? For the next thirty minutes, I was involved in the most frenzied and frustrating experience of my brief coaching career. Because the referee did not understand the importance of his call to leadership on the court, and because he had poor vision regarding how the game should be played, confusion reigned and eventually children were hurt.

In basketball, as in any other sport, officials are placed in their positions of authority to provide oversight. They are not charged with creating the rules of the game; rather, they are placed in their positions of leadership to set the general direction of the game, the tone of the game, the pace of the game, and enforce the rules of the game to ensure justice on the court and to protect players from injury.

Fundamentally, the official in this game had a flawed vision regarding his position on the court. He chose to *just let 'em play.* He didn't take charge. He did not understand the concept of positional power. Had the referee understood the significance of his position and used his position to add value to the game, there would have been less confusion, despair, and injustice on the court. Unfortunately, he did not understand the power and significance of his position.

The Court of Life

It is the same on the well-worn court of life. Position matters. From the time of his birth in a feeding trough to the time he ascended Mount Calvary, Jesus was consistent and powerful in his play. In all of his given positions, he was perfectly aligned with God's purpose, using the power of those positions to create value and influence in the world. His life was strategically lived in order to accomplish the goals his father had set before him. He never *just let 'em play*! Regardless of his position (son, student, carpenter, friend, citizen, teacher, or savior), he took charge and enhanced the play of those around him. His life made the lives of others better. Through his positions, he pointed others to God. Sometimes he did it publicly, like he did through the Sermon on the Mount. Sometimes he did it privately, like he did when he healed Peter's mother-in-law at home. Regardless, he knew his way around the court, and he used every dimension of God's power in his positions to get the job done.

Legends of the NBA understand. Larry Byrd, legendary Boston Celtics player, was asked to touch the ball at least once every twenty-four seconds.

Why? Because every time he touched the ball, he enhanced play on the basket-ball court. When he was given the ball, he made the game better for his team. Sometimes, he shot. Sometimes, he passed, or dribbled, or helped set up another play. Regardless, he always added value when he got the ball. That's why he is considered one of the greatest players ever!

Divine Appointment

As a leader, you often sense you are part of something larger than life—bigger than yourself. You feel that history is working uniquely through your position, providing you a rendezvous with destiny. Winston Churchill is often quoted as having said it this way, "There comes a special moment in everyone's life, a moment for which that person was born. That special opportunity, when he seizes it, will fulfill his mission—a mission for which he is uniquely qualified. In that moment, he finds greatness. It is his finest hour."

The day after his father's death, Bret Favre sensed his finest hour. He made the decision to go ahead and quarterback for his team, the Green Bay Packers, on Monday Night Football. While the media debated his decision to play, Favre delivered his greatest performance ever, throwing for 399 yards and 4 touch-downs to defeat the Broncos 35–12. When asked how he did it, Favre replied, "I gained an incredible sense of focus because I knew I was playing to honor my father on the world's largest playing field." Bret Favre sensed his positional role in destiny and played for the brand that night.

Here is the big idea! Your call to build a brand of living and leadership that matters is a divine appointment! It is divinely determined by God and is, therefore, huge.

This divine appointment is not solely for full-time clergy. In fact, most of Jesus' work was done with marketplace people. Have you ever stopped to think that none of the original twelve disciples was a leader in the synagogue or in the temple? The writing of the gospels was not entrusted to religious scholars but to marketplace leaders: a medical doctor (Luke), a retired tax officer (Matthew), a partner in a food enterprise (John), and an unemployed millionaire (Mark).[12] An unemployed millionaire!? Perhaps. Mark may have come from a very wealthy family. His mother, Mary, was the one in whose house many met to pray for Peter's release from prison.[13] Mary must have had a large home to accommo-date such a gathering. When Peter knocked at the gate, Rhoda, a maidservant, answered. Poor people did not have servants, and their homes did not have gates. Startled, Rhoda ran inside without opening the gate. Peter kept on knocking but was not heard by the other people inside Mary's house. This indicates that the house probably had a long entranceway, another indication of great wealth.[14]

Jesus himself was a businessperson with his father, Joseph. Matthew quotes a reference to Jesus as "the carpenter's son," using the Greek word "tekton, meaning "artificer, craftsman." Mark quotes a similar reference, which specifically refers to Jesus as a "carpenter," a tekton. Neither Joseph nor Jesus was a simple woodworker; they were craftsmen. By the time of Jesus' baptism, he had been working at his profession for many years. He was not a mere apprentice but a well-established artisan.

Jesus was divinely appointed and anointed in the marketplace! People ran to him when they saw him there. His best work was not done in the temple; it took place when he was out among the people. In fact, Scripture records that throughout the whole region of Gennesaret, the people "carried the sick on mats to wherever they heard he was. And wherever he went—into villages, towns or the countryside—they placed the sick in the marketplaces. They begged him to let them touch even the edge of his cloak, and all who touched him were healed."[15]

The marketplace is where people have always met Jesus. For this reason, Jesus utilized a vast array of teaching parables to show that he was intimately familiar with a variety of positions in the marketplace and operations management. His teaching examples dealt with the following:[16]

- Construction (Matt. 7:24–27)
- Wine making (Luke 5:37–38)
- Farming (Mark 4:2–20)
- Ranching (Matt. 18:12–14)
- Management and labor (Matt. 20:1–16)
- Family-owned businesses (Matt. 21:28–31)
- Hostile takeovers (Luke 20:9–19)
- Return on investments (Matt. 25:14–30)
- Crop yield (Mark 13:27–32)
- Management criteria (Luke 12:35–48)
- Misuse of money and bankruptcy (Luke 15:11–16)
- Advantage of leverage (Luke 16:1–13)

Positional leadership in the marketplace, not just the temple, is part of our call. Do you believe it? I do. Do you believe that you are a significant part of God's eternal leadership plan? I do.

———

God said to Abram, "Leave your country, your people and your father's household and go to the land I will show you."[17] Why did Abram get the call to leadership? There was confusion on the court. God needed Abram to use a nation to point people to Jesus—God told him, "through your offspring all nations on the earth will be blessed."[18]

Abram is on the fence post!

Joseph explained to his brothers that his positions in prison, in Pharaoh's house, and his civic positions in Egypt were all for a purpose. He said, ". . . it was to save lives that God sent me . . . ."[19] And, "God sent me ahead of you to preserve for you a remnant on earth and to save your lives by a great deliverance."[20] He has a rendezvous with God's destiny.

Like Abram, Joseph is on the fence post!

How about that? Could it be that we, too, like Joseph, are meant to save lives? Could it be that, like Joseph, God has sent us to preserve a remnant on earth and to save lives through a great deliverance? How did Joseph do it? He built a brand of leadership that mattered through distinctive living, empowered by the presence and purpose of God.

Esther used her position and relationships to add value when confusion reigned in the court of Xerxes. Haman brought danger to the Jews. Through the work of Mordecai, God sent a message to Esther that said, "who knows but that you have come to royal position for such a time as this?"[21]

Esther was on the fence post! God did it! I know you are in your positions, whatever they may be, for such a time as this.

The message seems clear. God will use his people to deliver this world from confusion, hurt, and bondage in a variety of ways. Clearly, Scripture speaks of his call to use our given positions to build his brand. I believe all Christians are divinely called to leadership, and that "God has arranged the parts of the body, every one of them, just as he wanted them to be" to accomplish his mission.[22] Unfortunately, the positions that seem to attract all of today's attention and effort are employee and employer. Yet other positions are also important.

Take the position of parent, for example. Many families have obvious dysfunction, brokenness, and abuse, while others look good on the outside but crumble from lack of attention on the inside. Parents in these situations may be strategically brilliant at the office but on the home front they have no vision, no goals, no plans, and rarely engage in training and development for their God-given positions as parents. I wonder, who is in charge?

As Dr. Kevin Lehman suggests, "Today's kids are unionized, and they've got a game plan to drive you up the wall. Some of the ankle-biter battalion have even graduated to emeritus status and are holding down the hormone group division. But you don't have to let them call the shots."[23] Research shows that parents who take charge in their homes are more likely to produce kids who are heroes! In a 2001 USA Today article, Marilyn Elias reported on the work of sociologist Samuel Oliner, co-author of The Altruistic Personality, who together with his wife Pearl "has studied 800 rescuers and 250 bystanders. Among key differences between those who acted and those who did nothing:

- Bystanders reported more physical punishment and verbal abuse from parents. Parents of rescuers were more likely to reason with children and explain how their actions might hurt others.
- Parents of rescuers were much more likely to be community volunteers and helpful to others. 'They model an ethic of caring,' Oliner says.
- Future heroes were exposed to more diverse people in their homes-- people of different religions, races and social classes
- And their families often had a spiritual tenor. 'They were Christians with a capital C, not the kind who came home and made racist remarks,' Oliner says.

Elizabeth Midlarsky, a Columbia University psychologist, has studied 98 Holocaust heroes, looking at how their families compared with those of neighbors who didn't step forward to help save lives. The heroes came from more affectionate homes, and every single one reported having role models, usually helpful people devoid of bigotry. Bystanders rarely said they had role models, Midlarsky says. Also, the families of future heroes did more activities together and spent more time talking, perhaps amplifying the parents' positive influence.

Heroes learn empathy and social responsibility at home, she says. 'They grow up to feel they must be their brother's keeper.'"[24]

So, if you are a parent, your position matters! Abandon the ordinary and build a brand of leadership that takes charge. Fulfill the obligations inherent in the position. Be a leader. Be a parent that makes an eternal difference. Engage in as much strategic planning and execution at home as you do at the office. Don't outsource the duties of parenthood. Seek the power of God's perspective, contemplate the power of his position, and lead your children to greatness.

The Only One

Jesus was given his position for one reason: God wanted to save the world.

Jesus was the only one for the job! His position was unique. Because he was sinless and not born of Adam, Jesus was the only one who could conquer him who held the power of death.[25] He had a divine rendezvous with destiny. He was on the fencepost! Without Jesus' position in the universe, salvation could not be attained. Jesus had all authority in heaven and on earth. It had been given to him.[26] If Jesus was not the sinless, perfect lamb of God, he would be under the dominion of Satan. However, since he obeyed his heavenly father and laid down his life for you and me, his position allows him to claim salvation for all mankind! If Jesus was simply a nice man or even a great prophet, salvation would not have been secured. Jesus had to have the positional power to defeat Satan, thereby providing a way of salvation for the rest of us. He was put in charge, so he took charge!

Publicity of Position

God used an interesting strategy regarding position. He publicly acknowledged the significance of positions. If you are like the centurion and have people under your authority (children, employees, church members, volunteers), do what God did for his son. Acknowledge their positions publicly, empowering them to see the significance of their positions and their work. Remember, when Jesus was beginning his ministry, God announced his arrival right after his baptism. "As soon as Jesus was baptized, he went up out of the water. At that moment heaven was opened, and he saw the Spirit of God descending like a dove and lighting on him. And a voice from heaven said, 'This is my son, whom I love; with him I am well pleased.'"[27] God was establishing Jesus and announcing and anointing the significance of his position among men.

In like fashion (albeit a bit less important and dramatic), I took my daughter to open her first bank account. As we began the conversation with the personal banker, I made it a point to say, "This is my daughter. I am really proud of her, and I support her having full access to her account as well as any account belonging to our family." This caught the personal banker off guard, but my intention was to publicly proclaim my pride and trust in her. She hasn't let us down.

God publicly announced the significance of Jesus' position to his closest followers because these would be the guys who would provide the foundation of leadership for Christianity after the resurrection. Listen, "After six days Jesus took with him Peter, James and John the brother of James, and led them up a high mountain by themselves. There he was transfigured before them. His face shown like the sun, and his clothes became as white as light. Just then there appeared before them Moses and Elijah, talking with Jesus. Peter said to Jesus, 'Lord, it is good for us to be here. If you wish, I will put up three shelters—one for you, one for Moses and one for Elijah.' While he was still speaking, a bright cloud enveloped them, and a voice from the cloud said, 'This is my Son, whom I love; with him I am well pleased. Listen to him!'"[28]

God took time to strategically acknowledge the significance of his son's position. Thus, it might be a good practice for you to take time to publicly acknowledge the significance of those under your watch: employees, children, colleagues, grandchildren, spouse, siblings, and friends. Public acknowledgment highlights the significance of their positions among their peers. It also highlights the significance of their positions in their own minds. They will know that you are cognizant of their positions, and they will more likely want to take charge because they have been put in charge!

A Great Myth

As we contemplate the call, let's not be confused ourselves. Position is part of the game, but it is definitely not the *object* of the game. Recognition of your position on the court and its inherent responsibility is the object of the game of life under God's sovereignty. Leadership is not about being at the top of an organization or being in the spotlight and on stage. Mistakenly, many people think leadership equals being the most notable among us. Why? Often it is because public figures are exalted as heroes who represent the true model of leadership.

However, as Joseph Badaracco points out in his book, *Leading Quietly*, "the most effective leaders are rarely public heroes. These men and women aren't high-profile champions of causes, and don't want to be . . . They move patiently, carefully, and incrementally. They do what is right—for their organizations, for the people around them, and for themselves—inconspicuously and without casualties."[29]

Terry Allen Hill wrote a great song that included the line, "Nobody wants to play rhythm guitar behind Jesus." In other words, everybody wants to be the *leader* of the band. But building a brand of leadership that matters is for all who have *position*—not just the *top* position.

We are all turtles on fence posts. We have no positions that were not granted to us. My position as a son was granted to me by my parents and the Lord. My position as a husband was granted to me by Jeanne, her folks, and the Lord. My position as a daddy was granted to me by Jeanne and the Lord. My position in public schools was granted to me by the superintendent and the Lord. My positions in college were granted to me by admissions personnel and the Lord. My first real job was granted to me by a human resource manager, who happened to be my brother (it pays to know people in the right places), and the Lord. My job as dean of the College of Business was granted to me by a search committee, the provost, the president, the board of trustees, and the Lord. None of these were things I could have obtained on my own.

God has placed each of us on the court of life in a variety of positions just where he needs us. Only when we realize we have each been given divine appointments will we build an exemplary brand of leadership that matters.

Key Points

1. When in charge, take charge.
2. We are all given multiple positions on the "court of life." Each different. Each important. Each in its own time. All have tremendous potential for adding value in the lives of those we love and lead.
3. Jesus knew who he was and understood the significance of his position on the "court of life." He was the only one who had the positional power to secure salvation for all people. Thankfully, Jesus did not just "just let 'em play."
4. One of the greatest abuses of power on the court of life is to forsake opportunities to create value inherent in the positions you have been given.
5. The official on the basketball court failed in his mission because he failed to see the significance of his position.
6. You have a rendezvous with God's destiny: to build a brand of leadership that matters.
7. Publicly acknowledging those under your influence, a behavior modeled by God, empowers those under your leadership and influence to see the significance of their given positions.

Challenge

Perhaps I am becoming a bit cynical as I grow older, but increasingly I witness numerous people who squander incredible potential in their positions to make a difference. They simply don't reach their potential. They are put in charge, but they don't take charge. I often ask myself why. I am not sure I have a brilliant answer, but I think it has something to do with the way people see themselves and the importance of their positions. Too many college students I work with don't see what I see in them. I see great potential. They seem oblivious to the possibilities. I often feel like Andy Williams at Christmas time, asking them, "Do you see what I see?"

Growing up, I was never overtly taught to make a difference. I was more often taught to stay away from evil and the world. The teaching and approach is fundamentally sound but it lacks completeness. Thus, I rarely viewed the positions I had as opportunities to make a difference for the Lord. I simply tried to live right within them. Of course you make a difference by living right. But there is so much more!

Due to my experience at that early YMCA basketball game and my years of coaching involvement with my daughters and their sports activities, I can tell you that excellent sports officials make an extraordinary difference in any game played. Great officials add value by creating the frameworks for great games of contest. They define the rules. They take charge and establish authority.

Great fathers and mothers add value by creating the frameworks for greatness in their homes. They set the tone of the family early on in life. They define the rules. They set the vision. They take charge and establish authority. They know they have been put in charge by a higher authority. Thus, they take charge! It pains me when I see children boss their parents around. I know the children are destined for failure because the parents failed to step up to the plate.

Would it be too much of a stretch to say that your job is a position with divine purposes? What type of person might you be if you believed your position was given directly by God? Would you pay more attention to your performance? This one big idea could change your life for eternity.

Exploring Big Ideas

1. In general, why do you think people fail to take charge in their positions?

2. Note all your given positions on the "court of life" in all realms: workplace, home, family, church, community, etc. Describe how you might take charge in these positions.

3. Describe times when Jesus took charge. What caused him to take action as he did?

4. How could you enhance your ability to take charge in your positions on the "court of life"?

5. Do you think people, in general, think of themselves as having been divinely appointed to their current positions in life? Why? Why not?

6. Why don't we publicly acknowledge people more often?

7. What does public acknowledgement do for those who are being acknowledged AND for those who hear the proclamation?

Chapter Five

What's the Big Idea?

All things that are worthwhile begin with an idea.
To have an idea for which you are fighting
is fundamental to leadership.

—Benjamin Netanyahu, prime minister of Israel

On April 9, 2003, Benjamin Natanyahu solidified the next principle for me, and this is the big idea I want to share.

I was privileged to be involved in a private conference call conversation with Mr. Netanyahu, prime minister of Israel, and eight CEOs of U.S.-based companies. I called in from a house on Beaver Lake near Siloam Springs, Arkansas, moved again by the beauty of the water and the passion of Mr. Netanyahu's words.

"All things worthwhile begin with an idea," Mr. Netanyahu said. "It is ideas you fight for. To have an idea for which you are fighting is fundamental to leadership."

The entire conversation revolved around leadership and its foundational relationship to ideas, particularly those he was passionately fighting for in his home country, Israel.

"All ethical leadership involves confronting the naysayers and taking the risk to defend the idea," he said.

I'll never forget this truth I learned that day from a passionate leader and statesman: ideas are fundamental to leadership! Ideas make that which is formless and empty have life! Ideas shape the future.

———

Ideas are fundamental to building a distinctive brand of living and leadership. Before the idea of the wheel, there was no wheel. Before the idea of the cross, there was no forgiveness of sin. No big idea, no set of distinctive brand promises. No big idea, no power to connect with people. No big idea, no ability to create value and influence in the lives of those you love and lead. No big idea, no leadership that matters.

Thus, ideas are marks of your brand.

They are a distinct set of ideas and promises strategically crafted to create a brand of leadership that matters.

Now consider God's big idea.

Everything that now is, was once impossible. The world as we know it, everything that exists, began as an idea in the mind of God. At one time, heaven and earth did not exist. Today heaven and earth exist because God had an idea and, in the beginning, God created! At first, things were formless and empty. Then God's ideas began to forge distinction: light, darkness, morning, evening—a day. What a great idea!

Consider life without morning and evening—a day. No closure. No rest. No anticipation. No new starts. No stars. No dew. No sunrise. No sunset. No evening walks. No lying down at night. No nighttime prayers. But God had an idea. The very breath of God created. The Scriptures eloquently paint a word picture of the power of God's ideas in creation: how he thought about it, planned it, engineered it, and made it happen.

Ideas are the substructure and power grid that sustain and carry life. Ideas are to human behavior what respiration is to life. They are an essential phenomenon, the driving force behind human endeavor. In the simple but elegant words of Solomon, "Where there is no vision [no idea], the people perish."[1]

———

Long before men conquered mountains, an idea about mountains conquered men. Years ago, men believed that the gods lived in the mountains. This fundamental idea caused every high mountain to be idolized by the people living in its shadow. For example, inspired by the majesty of the Himalayas, Hindus and Buddhists imagined a mythical 84,000 mile-high mountain above the mountains to be the dwelling place of their gods. The Japanese had their Fujiyama, a goddess who dominated the landscape and never ceased to be celebrated in their art. In the West, the Greeks had their Olympus, abruptly rising nearly 9,000 feet above the Aegean Sea.

The Greeks were certain that Mt. Olympus was the highest point on earth and that it was home to the gods. It was thought that Zeus and other gods made Olympus their eternal residence. Daniel J. Boorstin describes this in his book, *The Discoverers*: "Often shrouded in clouds, the veiled summit of Olympus gave gods their privacy. Only between the clouds could mortals glimpse an amphitheater of tiers of boulders where the gods sat in council. 'Never is it swept by the winds nor touched by snow,' wrote Homer, 'a purer air surrounds it, a white clarity envelops it and the gods there taste of a happiness which lasts as long as their eternal lives.'"[2]

And on the heights of Mt. Sinai, the God of Abraham, Isaac, and Jacob gave Moses the tablets of the law—the Ten Commandments. Moses was told that he was not to touch the mountain because it was holy and anyone who touched it would die. Thus, it seemed clear to the Jews and Moses that God lived in the mountain.

The idea that mountains were links between heaven and earth caused generations of men to build artificial mountains where there were none. The oldest surviving examples are the stepped pyramids—the "ziggurats"—of ancient Mesopotamia, which date back to nearly 3000 BC. The Tower of Babel, the Egyptian pyramids in lower Egypt (2980 BC), and the Hindu and Buddhist temples of India all became a symbol of man's effort to reach the heavens based on his idea that mountains were the gods' dwelling places.[3]

The ziggurat was said to be the earthly shape of the ladder that Jacob saw in Genesis 28:12: "And he dreamed, and behold a ladder set up on the earth, and the top of it reached to heaven: and behold the angels of God ascending and descending on it." Every major city in Mesopotamia had at least one high-reaching ziggurat to allow the gods to reach down more easily to men. Though the idea was perhaps flawed, its imprint on human behavior remains to this day.

I marvel at the significant and ordered relationship between big ideas and life as we know it. Perhaps I marvel because I rarely have a big idea. Think about the ideas of conception and birth. Could you have imagined such a process?

What about marriage? Would you have designed it that way? Would you have made it so complicated? Could you have made the process of raising children a little less intense and difficult? Would forgiveness be one of your creative ideas? I wonder if your big idea list would have contained this one: reconciliation to a holy God by grace through a son's obedience and death on an old rugged cross!

Once you begin to ponder, it is easy to see that ideas are fundamental to life as we know it. It is also easy to see that ideas are manifestations of the creator within us. For example, mankind has had some pretty cool ideas that have manifested over the years: the wheel, electricity, the printing press, the thermometer, the lightbulb, contact lenses, surgery, vaccinations, the automobile, the airplane, the Segway, the personal computer, the Internet, mobile data devices, a forty-hour work week, and vacations, to name a few.

These ideas have dramatically impacted the way we live on earth. Consider your life as impacted by technology. Today, in the palm of your hand, many of you process email, make telephone calls, watch movies, send text messages, play music, search the Internet, obtain stock quotes, retrieve weather forecasts, play games, and read the Bible because Steve Jobs and company contemplated a big idea and called it the iPhone. Some people do not value innovation, creativity, and the limitless power of ideas. I am amused by the myopic statement of Mr. Charles H. Duell, U.S. Commissioner of Patents in 1899, who said, "Everything that can be invented has been invented." Clearly not!

Nations also manifest ideas. Nations exhibit the ideas that shape them at any given time. The founders of the United States deployed significant and magnificent ideas: faith in God, religious freedom, freedom of speech, private ownership, tri-lateral government, free enterprise, democracy of the people for the people and by the people, public education, and federal income tax, to name a few. I am not sure taxes were such a great idea, come to think of it. Though these ideas pale in comparison with God's, they define us as a people. They shape us and structure life as we know it today. Certainly, they have fundamentally changed our world. These ideas have provided leadership for our nation since 1776 and continue to do so today.

Eleanor Roosevelt once said, "Great minds discuss ideas; average minds discuss events; small minds discuss people."[4] Is yours a "great mind?" What are you discussing on a daily basis? What are the big ideas in your life that you are fighting for? With great ideas come great distinction in living and leadership.

A Symphony of Ideas

Dr. Henry Mintzberg, a well-known management theorist and scholar, suggested that leadership may best be understood by examining what the leader is seeing. He suggests that leadership is as much about ideas as it is about the analytics of specific strategies and implementation. Mintzberg, for years, has suggested that management teams must focus on unique visions and ideas that create a sense of destiny and direction for their companies.[5] The great composer Mozart said, "the best part about creating a symphony is being able to *see* the whole of it at a single glance in my mind."[6] Mozart's words speak to the relationship between ideas and vision—the summary picture of the piece of work—and performance.

Mintzberg and Mozart support the findings of Collins and Porras who discovered that companies with visionary CEOs outperformed the general stock market by a 15:1 ratio.[7] These CEOs were extraordinary leaders because they had a guiding set of ideas, a vision, a blueprint that led to their companies' greatness. Similarly, authors Baum, Locke, and Kirkpatrick found that small entrepreneurial companies with great vision displayed considerably higher performance than those without vision.[8]

Are you ready to think and discuss big ideas with your friends, family, church, company?

In the remainder of this chapter, I will share some simple yet profound "big ideas" behind some of the best brands in the world today.

They Took a Great Idea and Made It Fly

In 1971, Rollin King and Herb Kelleher got together and decided to start a different kind of airline. They began with one simple idea: If you get your passengers to their destinations when they want to get there, on time, at the lowest possible fares, and make sure they have a good time doing it, people will fly your airline.

And you know what? They were right. What began as a small Texas airline has grown to become one of the largest airlines in America, Southwest Airlines, flying over 104 million passengers a year to 64 cities, 3,400 times per day, all across the United States. Since 1987, when the Department of Transportation began tracking Customer Satisfaction statistics, Southwest has consistently led the entire airline industry with the lowest ratio of complaints per passengers boarded. One big idea. One distinctive airline.

Imagination at Work

In 1892, Thomas Alva Edison founded The General Electric Company (GE). Since that time, GE has been built on the power of one big idea: bringing good things to life. Edison wanted his inventions to help people. He is quoted as saying, "I never perfected an invention that I did not think about in terms of the service it might give to others."[9] For nearly 120 years, GE has continued innovation for the good of other people.

From 1981 to 2001, GE was led by Mr. John F. Welch, Jr. (Jack), heralded in 1999 by *Fortune* magazine to be the "Manager of the Century" and, recently, by the *Financial Times* to be one of the three most admired business leaders in the world today.[10] In 1980, the year before Welch became CEO, GE recorded revenues of roughly $26.8 billion; in 2000, the year before he left, they were nearly $130 billion. The company went from a market value of $14 billion to one of more than $410 billion at the time of his retirement, making it the most valuable and largest company in the world.

Jack Welch had one big idea during his tenure at GE: "Search out and participate in the real growth industries and insist upon being number one or number two in every business—the number one or number two leanest, lowest cost, worldwide producers of quality goods and services."[11] What an incredibly simple but powerful idea!

Eat More Chicken

Credited with introducing the boneless chicken breast sandwich, Chik-fil-A, Inc., is one of the largest privately held restaurant chains in the United States today. The famous national chain of fast food restaurants operates according to two big ideas:

1. Glorify God by being a faithful steward of all that is entrusted to them.
2. Have a positive influence on all who come in contact with Chik-fil-A.

These two big ideas have resulted in 1,428 restaurants (as of February 2009) in 38 states and Washington, D.C. Every location is closed on Sunday, as has been the case for more than fifty years, though Sunday is one of the two biggest retailing days of the week.

Of the more than three billion dollars in annual revenues, a major portion goes to help others. The WinShape Centre foundation sponsors foster homes, a scholarship program at Berry College, and Camp WinShape, a summer program that annually attracts more than fifteen hundred campers. Additionally, the Chik-fil-A Bowl leads all bowl games in charitable donations, giving more than a million dollars to charities each year and, to date, tens of thousands of its restaurant employees receive scholarships to institutions of higher learning. Chik-fil-A is unique because the ideas of the owners are unique. They place their faith in Jesus and use their big ideas to make a daily difference in a big way![12]

The Language of Refreshment

Robert Goizueta, former chairman of Coca-Cola, once asked a series of powerful questions of his senior managers at an annual leadership retreat. They struggled to see his whole vision at one time, but he wanted his company to grow. He knew that the common idea among his management team was that Coca-Cola dominated the beverage market. Indeed, many felt it impossible to gain more market share.

Goizueta began the exploration by asking his management team this question: "What is our current market share?"

They responded in unison: "Forty-five percent!"

He asked, "On average, how many ounces of liquid does a human being drink each day?"

They responded, but a bit puzzled, "Sixty-four ounces per day."

Goizueta asked, "On average, how many ounces of all of our products does a person drink per day?"

The managers responded a bit more timidly with bewilderment, "Two ounces."

Then he asked, "Now, what is our market share?"

The senior management team at Coca-Cola had one idea of who they were in the marketplace. Goizueta had another. Management understood its market share to be forty-five percent. Goizueta understood it to be three percent.

With a shift to that one big idea, Goizueta dramatically changed the way Coca-Cola did business then and the way it does business today. Coca-Cola managers had assumed that traditional soft drink markets were saturated. They had assumed that the company couldn't grow rapidly, and that any growth it could get would come from buying other businesses.

However, by moving away from the idea that the competition was not PepsiCo, and instead seeing the competition as any other beverage on the market, Goizueta unleashed the energy of Coca-Cola's managers to search for growth opportunities everywhere in the world. Mr. Goizueta's big idea allowed Coca-Cola to experience rapid growth, building marketing strategies using per capita consumption metrics by global region and nation. Coca-Cola now owns four of the five top nonalcoholic sparkling beverage brands in the world, serving refreshment to people of many languages in more than 200 nations 1.5 billion times per day.[13] Since 1886, they remain one of the most valued companies on earth.

A People's Car

On January 17, 1934, Dr. Ferdinand Porsche presented his big ideas to Adolf Hitler, who had previously commissioned him to create a "people's car" for the nation of Germany. Porsche demanded that a "volks" (people) "wagen" (car) create a new manifesto for a new motoring era. "A people's car must not be a miniature version of an automobile with reduced dimensions likely to affect its handling, performance and operating life," he wrote. He went on to say,

> Yet with relatively high weight—an objective which can be achieved only by completely new methods. In the same way, a people's car must not be a small car with a body offering limited occupant and luggage space and sacrificing ride comfort; instead, it should be a practical means of transportation with body styles providing normal and thus comfortable accommodation. A people's car, furthermore, must not be a vehicle with a limited range of applications: instead, simple interchange of bodies should suffice to render it suitable for all probable purposes—not only as a private car but also as a goods delivery vehicle or for certain military functions. A people's car must not be burdened with complex equipment calling for an increased level of maintenance, but should instead be a vehicle with equipment designed to be as foolproof as possible, and with all forms of maintenance reduced to a practicable minimum.[14]

Boy, did Porsche deliver! Through his unique idea, he created one of the most notable cars still on the road today: the Volkswagen Beetle. Today, every adult in a developed nation is familiar with Porsche's "bug" because of its distinctive design and enduring character. More than forty million have been produced to date!

Dr. Porsche, a man of ideas, vision, and passion, was a distinctive learner. He once visited a construction yard in Europe to assess progress at the site. In the yard, he encountered three different yard workers at three different times throughout the day. He asked a worker on his first encounter to explain the nature of his job. The worker explained that he was a common laborer. "I work until they tell me to stop working. Then I go home and take orders from no one," the worker replied. Later in the day, Porsche asked a second worker in the yard to explain what he did. The second worker replied, "I am a bricklayer. I have been laying brick for thirty years, and I am tired."

Near the end of the day, Porsche spotted a worker who continued to exhibit great enthusiasm. Porsche asked him what it was he did at the construction site. The third worker replied, "I build cathedrals!" In reality, each of the workers had the same job at the construction site; only one had a vision of how the labor of his hands was contributing to greatness. Thus, he approached his work with passion and a sense of meaning. You can bet his work was peppered with excellence and distinction.

Ferrying Spare Parts

During his days as a student at Yale University in the 1960s, Fred W. Smith hired himself out as a charter pilot. While flying students and other passengers around, he noticed that he was frequently ferrying spare parts for computer companies such as IBM. These companies didn't want to wait on passenger airlines to get critical components to customers. Smith, an economics major, formulated his idea in 1965 and wrote a term paper about it for one of his classes. Legend has it that he received a "C" on the paper. Smith can't remember the grade, but states, "I knew the idea was profound."[15]

His idea hit home with a variety of capital investors who provided more than eighty million dollars to set up Federal Express Corporation in 1971. Smith's big idea guaranteed overnight delivery of critical goods between any two points in the eleven-city network he created. His first night's run had seven packages. He expanded his network to 25 cities and re-launched his service a month later— this time handling a grand total of 186 packages. In 2009, FedEx generated 35.5

billion dollars in annual revenues and is still the biggest operator of its class, with a forty-four percent market share of the air express market. Its fleet of nearly 700 aircraft and 71,000 trucks carry an average of 5.5 million shipments each day, and all because a college kid had a big idea!

Interchangeability of Parts

In their classic business book, *The Machine that Changed the World*, MIT authors James P. Womack, Daniel T. Jones, and Daniel Roos explain how Henry Ford changed the world through his idea of mass production. "The key to mass production wasn't—as many people then and now believe—the moving, or continuous, assembly line. Rather, it was the complete and consistent interchangeability of parts and the simplicity of attaching them to each other. These were the manufacturing innovations [ideas] that made the assembly line possible."[16] During Ford's day, automobiles were built by craftsmen in one location on the shop floor. The system was much like one you would use today to build a model airplane in your workshop—the model airplane remains stationary while you mobilize handcrafted parts and bring them to the table for assembly.

However, once Ford came up with the idea that a variety of parts could be machined within strict tolerances, he figured that any particular part on one vehicle could be interchanged with its counterpart on any other vehicle. With this idea came the advent of the assembly line. Ford visualized mass automobile production via an assembly line where vehicles moved along a path and stationary workers fit interchangeable parts into each car as it arrived at their work stations. From this one idea came a system of manufacturing and production that allowed Ford Motor Company to sell the Model T in 1908 to common folk for the modest price of five hundred dollars while paying factory workers five dollars per day—more than double the average auto worker's salary—to produce them.

Conclusion

Building a distinctive brand of leadership that matters begins with distinctive ideas. Distinctive leaders find the big ideas and then fight for them. What big ideas are determining the way you lead at the office? Are you generic, leading like all the other people do? What about in your home? Are you deploying distinctive ideas to bless your family? And in your church? What will your ideas there accomplish?

Remember, ideas are the sub-structure of greatness. Someone once said that vision is seeing what everybody has seen, but thinking what nobody has thought. Visions and ideas are defining. They define God. They define us. They define life. They define leadership.

Key Points

1. All things that are worthwhile begin with an idea.
2. Ideas are the sub-structure of life as we know it.
3. Everything that now is was once impossible. The world began as an idea in the mind of God.
4. To have an idea for which you are fighting is fundamental to leadership.
5. Great minds discuss ideas.
6. What you see determines who you will be.
7. Distinctive brands, distinctive lives, and distinctive families result from distinctive ideas!

Challenge

What ideas are you thinking about today? Your ideas don't have to be featured on the nightly news to be important. Seriously, do you know what ideas you're fighting for? Have you taken time to contemplate some big ideas in marriage, parenting, church, your profession, and in your community? God says he has plans for you, "plans to prosper you and not to harm you."[17] So what plans do you have?

Many university students don't ask any tough questions regarding their degree plans other than, "Is this class easy?" They simply ask advisors to tell them what courses they need to take. Thus, most students end up with an average experience in college. Nothing in their program makes them distinctive because they follow a general plan established by someone else. When they seek to explore the idea of distinctiveness in their college work, they can invest in the numerous growth opportunities available.

The idea here is that, in reality, everyone follows a plan! You may not know it, but you make decisions each day according to some idea of what is appropriate for you. The nagging questions to contemplate remain: Are you following your own plan? Is it a great plan? Does it lead to distinction in living and leadership for you, your family, your church, your business, or your community? If yours is not a plan of greatness, ask yourself, why not? If you are not working on your own big ideas, ask yourself, whose big ideas are you using? Are you simply reflecting society's plan? Are you adopting your neighbor's plan? Do you seem to be living very much like your coworkers? Or like the pictures offered by

Hollywood? Get with it! You need big ideas that are distinct and powerful, building a brand of leadership that has power to change what really matters!

Exploring Big Ideas

1. Tell of a time when a big idea made a significant difference in your life. Explain the idea, and describe the result.

2. Describe the importance of ideas. Then, describe the ideas you are using to build your life.

3. Do your ideas point to greatness, to distinctive living, and to leadership? Why or why not?

4. What prohibits us from using big ideas to guide our lives?

5. How would you describe the idea of the cross? Was it a great idea?

6. Why do you think great leaders have an idea that their lives are a part of some greater good, a sense of some greater destiny? Do you have a sense of destiny within you? Look up John 15:16 and see if you might have been chosen for greatness.

7. How do you go about obtaining the big ideas necessary to build a brand that matters?

Chapter Six

MORE THAN SHADOWS ON A CAVE WALL

If your eyes are good,
your whole body will be full of light.
—MATTHEW 6:22

I n *The Republic*, Plato tells of men trapped in an underground chamber like a cave. They have been prisoners since they were children and their legs and necks are so stiff that they can only look straight ahead of them, unable to turn their heads. Fire burns behind and above them. Men carry all sorts of gear in front of the fire, making shadows on the cave wall. They *see* only an illusion or a shadow of reality that is projected on the wall of the cave. When one of the prisoners escapes to the upper world and discovers the truth—a world illuminated by sunlight—he attempts to go back and tell those in the cave what he sees. Because they think he is delusional, they kill him.

The cave dwellers' idea of reality determines who they become. The shadows on the wall, though only reflecting a fuller reality, drives their behavior. Because their eyes cannot see reality, they subject their lives to a miserable existence inside an underground chamber filled with darkness and fear.

Shadows of the Neanderthal

David Hutchens re-creates and illuminates the powerful, timeless ideas delivered in Plato's "Allegory of the Cave" in his own book, *Shadows of the Neanderthal*. In Hutchens' expanded narrative, Unga, Bunga, Oogie, Boogie, and Trevor live in

69

a cave.[1] In fact, they never leave the cave. They just stay in the cave, day in and day out, waiting for dead bugs and dried leaves to blow in so that they might have something to eat. The cave people embrace this isolated lifestyle because they believe the mouth of the cave is the edge of the universe. When Boogie first contemplates the idea of going outside the cave, Unga preaches, "Outside of cave is nothing. Go outside and *poof*—no more Unga." Bunga counters, "No, outside is big dragon. Dragon swallow Bunga whole." Oogie, another cave dweller, reasons, "Outside is big mad god. Big mad god stomp on Oogie, and splat, big gross mess."

Despite their cognitive differences, the cave friends are united in *one idea*: never leave the cave. They cower from the shadows on the back wall. To the men, these wall shadows were reality. "The cave people never realized how limited their understanding of the world was. For them, it was just truth. And they were satisfied."

One day, Boogie gets restless:

Looking around the same old drab walls of the cave, he casually mused, "Boogie wonder what is outside cave."

The others stared in shocked disbelief. No one had ever said such a thing before.

Boogie tried to explain: "Boogie just wonder if maybe more food outside. Or maybe more water. Or more room." . . .

"*Plenty* room here!" snapped Bunga.

"And plenty food," added Trevor, sucking on a rock.

"But we only see what inside cave," Boogie said. "What if we not see what really is?"

Boogie's friends are upset and angry. They think Boogie has lost his mind. Boogie's friends call him names and throw rocks and sticks at him, and they send him out of the cave. Boogie leaves the cave and experiences the bright light of the world outside.

As he lies crying from the vicious physical and verbal attacks of his cave friends, he looks up and sees the beauty of the outside world: trees, animals, rivers, blue sky, and lots and lots of other caves. It was far beyond his former, limited perspective. Boogie happens across Mike, a purveyor of truth and wisdom who knows Boogie has come from a cave because his grammar is so atrocious. Mike shows Boogie why so many people live in caves.

Mike explains a tale of two tribes and how they came to deal with food scarcity in their land. The elders of the land told the people to build two tall towers that would allow them to see as much of the surrounding land as possible. Accordingly, each tribe approached the elders with different conclusions based upon what they *saw*. The conclusions were substantively different. "We must build collecting baskets and storehouses for food and weaving looms to make tents," announced one group. "Only then will we be able to survive in the surrounding lands." But then another group spoke up: "No, we must build spears, traps, and tools for the hunt. Only then will we be able to survive in the surrounding lands."

They strongly disagreed. Consequently, they argued contentiously, trying to explain their prescribed recommendations. They called each other names like "barbarians, cowards, violent animals, and tree-hugging dorks!" These exchanges remind Boogie of his last moments in the cave. The people failed to reach consensus. Thus, they all went their own ways and built more caves for safe dwelling. Boogie can't understand why people disagree so violently, so Mike shows him the ancient towers that the peoples built long ago.

One tower faces west. The view from this tower holds beautiful fertile farmland teaming with grapevines, cotton bushes, and corn. The other tower faces east. The view from this tower holds a land that is rugged and rocky, populated with wild game. Boogie finally realizes that the people fought because the view from their particular towers resulted in different ideas for survival.

Their visions were limited, knowing only what they had seen *from their particular tower*. They could not comprehend a view from the other tower, nor could they comprehend the meaning of such an idea. Boogie's heart aches with sadness and fear, because he remembers the quality of life as he knew it in the cave. He decides to go back to his friends Oogie, Unga, Bunga, and Trevor and tries to explain his newly acquired vision of reality. They think he is delusional and refuse to listen. Instead, they throw sticks and stones at him and call him names. He is forever banished from the cave.

Shadows of the Neanderthal illuminates a salient point: we all live in caves, utilizing our own ideas to process what we *see* or what we *think we see*. Everyone's ideas are based only on what he or she knows. We only know what we know. The only way out of the cave is exposure to truth that is beyond us.

Jesus said that our eyes determine what we see. He said, "The eye is the lamp of the body. If your eyes are good, your whole body will be full of light. But if your eyes are bad, your whole body will be full of darkness. If then the light within you is darkness, how great is that darkness!"[2] If our eyes see good things, then our bodies are full of light. I think Jesus is saying that your ideas about life and living are functions of your vision. If your vision is good, your life will be framed by that which is good. If your vision is bad, your frame of reference will be tainted and will cause you to fall into harm and ruin.

When we are able to develop the vision of Jesus, climbing his tower and gaining his limitless view, we will see what he wants us to see and be what he wants us to be.

A Narrow and Wide Gate

One night several years ago our daughter, Hannah, then eleven years old, helped me understand the Lord's teaching on the wide and narrow gates. Our whole family was gathered in the bedroom of our youngest daughter, Michelle, for a pre-bedtime Bible reading. We were tired. It was late. We had just read Jesus' teaching in Matthew 7:7–12 on "asking and seeking" the night before. That night, I read Matthew 7:13–14, where Jesus spoke about the narrow and wide gates. As I closed the reading, I asked if anyone knew what it meant and if they could relate it to Jesus' teaching from the night before?

Hannah immediately raised her hand, as she often does. Her interpretation astounded me. "What Jesus meant is similar to people who want to drive up a mountain," she explained. "Most people notice the road that everyone else is taking to the top. It is usually a big, wide road that has lots of cars on it. But Daddy," she said, "usually, if you look real close, you can see a tiny little trail off to the side of the road. If you take this trail, you will not be bothered by lots of people and you will be able to see more flowers along the way. Plus, Daddy, once you get to the top, the view is much better than the view from the big road!"

Wow! God was really speaking through Hannah that night! She understood the big idea! In essence, she knew the small trail afforded better opportunities. I thanked her for her keen insight.

Again, she blurted out, "Daddy, I have another example!"

"Tell us," I said.

"It's like when people want to go fishing," she continued. "Most people go where all the other people are fishing on the side of the big road by the big river. They think that is where all the good fish are. But, if you look really hard, you can usually see a small river off in the woods. If you can get to the small river, there are bigger fish that are better tasting in cleaner water in the stream in the woods."

"That is really good, honey!" I said.

"Wait, Daddy."

"Yes?"

"The reason people don't come to the small river is that they don't *believe* there are any fish in there. The people who come must *believe* that they will find fish in the small river."

At that hour of the night, I knew for certain that God had spoken through my little girl. Thank you, God, for the insight of little children!

Hannah was saying, God's reality determines who you will be: distinctive or ordinary. Most people focus on what is easy to see (the main road, the big river). They draw their blueprints and ideas by climbing the commonly used towers. They really don't care to look carefully because they don't believe Jesus has anything special or distinctive to offer (there are no fish in that stream).

Philosopher and baseball great Yogi Berra said, "You can observe a lot by watching." How can we understand our current environment? Watch. A deeply ingrained characteristic of distinctive leaders is their passion for examining their current environments and continuously monitoring each ebb and flow.

John McPhee in his book, *A Sense of Where You Are*, tells the following story to illustrate the power of observation. It was 1965:

> . . . the floor of Princeton University gym was being resurfaced, so [basketball star Bill Bradley] had to put in several practice sessions at the Lawrenceville School. His first afternoon at Lawrenceville, he began by shooting fourteen-foot jump shots from the right side. He got off to a bad start, and he kept missing. Six in a row hit the back of the rim of the basket and bounced out. He stopped, looked discomfited, and seemed to be making an adjustment in his mind. Then he went up for another jump shot from the same spot and hit it cleanly. Four more shots went

without a miss, and then he paused and said, "You want to know something? That basket is about an inch and a half low."

Some weeks later, I went back to Lawrenceville with a steel tape, borrowed a stepladder, and measured the height of the basket. It was nine feet ten and seven-eighth inches above the floor, or one and one-eighth of an inch too low.

Amazing. Most of us attribute missed shots to a variety of reasons like having a bad day, sore muscles, or shooting in a new gym. Bradley didn't. His skill and ability to observe his environment allowed him to make the adjustment he needed.[3]

Environmental analysis or knowing your surroundings is the forerunner of distinctive ideas and blueprints. Most of the time, people don't take time to observe what is going on around them. They get too busy and forget the importance of observation. It is just easier to hustle and accomplish objectives. However, a good dose of reality will show us, as futurist and *Megatrends* author John Naisbitt points out, "The most reliable way to anticipate the future is by understanding the present."[4]

As noted earlier, General Electric, under the leadership of Jack Welch, had one of the most remarkable market capitalization growth patterns of any global company. One contributing factor is a fundamental corporate rule deployed by Welch. In his words, all distinctive leaders "must face reality as it is, not as it was or as you wish it were." Facing reality is crucial in life, not just in business. "You have to see the world in the purest, clearest way possible, or you can't make decisions on a rational basis."[5]

Likewise, Jim Collins says that all great leaders confront the brutal facts of their current reality. When leaders start with a diligent effort to determine the truth of their situations, the right decisions often become self-evident. For sure, it is impossible to make good decisions without infusing the entire process with an honest confrontation of the brutal facts.[6] Collins suggests four basic practices to help define reality:

1. Lead with questions, not answers.
2. Engage in dialogue and debate, not coercion.
3. Conduct autopsies, without blame.

4. Build red-flag mechanisms that turn information into information that cannot be ignored.[7]

The job of defining reality is not for cowards. It is difficult, at best, even for seasoned professionals. Consider the crew of a jet airliner, taking off from New York City. Noting surprisingly high airspeed readouts, the puzzled crew attributed them to unusual updrafts. They did not realize that before takeoff they had missed a crucial checklist item: turning on heaters to prevent freeze-up in the airspeed indicators. So the pilot kept easing back on the throttles to get the speed down.

When the control stick began to shake, the crew interpreted it as a "Mach buffet"—an indication they were approaching the speed of sound. It was actually a stall warning. These were professional pilots, trained to know the difference in a highly technical environment. But by the time the crewmembers recognized their error, their aircraft was plunging to the ground, hopelessly out of control. "Cabin and crew were both destroyed."[8] The costs of misreading a situation can be deadly—in an airplane, a business, a family, a church, or government.

Understanding Reality: An Environmental Analysis

As a distinctive leader, you must identify each of the positions you have been given (child, sibling, spouse, parent, employer, employee, church member, civic leader, soccer coach, etc.) and make sure you understand the landscape, the dynamic forces that shape life, and the future in that sector. In short, you need to conduct an authentic environmental analysis. A good environmental analysis comprises eight essential elements, which you can see in Table 6.1. These elements will help you define your specific reality so you can draft your distinctive blueprint and brand of leadership.

TABLE 6.1	
Essential Elements for Understanding Your Current Reality	
1. Climbing New Towers	5. Understanding Static Cling
2. Walking Where Others Walk	6. Feedback: The Breakfast of Champions
3. Reading, Reading, Reading	7. Reflecting on Your Past
4. Active Learning & Experience	8. Pray, Pray, Pray

Climbing New Towers

First, using the language of Mike and Boogie, you must be a lifelong tower climber! Staying in your cave will prohibit greatness. You must get out, climbing as many towers as you can to gain a full perspective of the landscape around you. Analyzing the forces that create your environment will allow you to capture great ideas and eventually cast great vision.

In Appendix A, you will find Worksheet 1, Environment Analysis, Part I (see p. 186), which you can use to develop a "new tower" perspective for each of your God-given positions of leadership. This worksheet will enable you to begin to record, prioritize, and analyze each of your divine leadership appointments. Before you begin using Worksheet 1, write each of your identified leadership positions on a separate sheet of paper (i.e. daughter, son, mother, father, sister, brother, husband, wife, friend, grandmother, grandfather, aunt, uncle, employee, employer, elder, deacon, pastor, etc.).

Once you have developed your list, rank order each position in terms of its current leadership priority for you. As you prioritize, think about the positions you hold that are most important according to your values and those positions that afford you the maximum influence. Prioritize the top five leadership positions that you desire to work on. Record these on Worksheet 1.

In business, an environmental analysis consists of continuously identifying and examining the forces that affect the nature of business and the future of business in a given marketplace, such as economic, geographic, demographic, sociocultural, political, and natural forces. By analyzing these forces, you can create sound strategies to deal with these realities and reach the goals of the organization.

Likewise, you can perform an environmental analysis for your role as mom, dad, wife, husband, sister, brother, elder, preacher, etc. While examining your family situation, for example, you will typically consider social, political, economic, family, educational, and extracurricular forces. So an environmental analysis for your position as parent may look like this:

Internal Family Forces: positive (+) or negative (-)
1. Time pressures due to dual income household (-)
2. Financial pressures due to children's educational and lifestyle expenses (-)

3. Poor physical and spiritual diet because of overextended lifestyles (-)
4. Little, if any, family time (-)
5. Sibling rivalry (-)
6. Behavioral challenges with any particular child (-)
7. Romantic malaise in marriage (-)
8. Lots of love in the home (+)
9. Good health for all family members (+)
10. A spirit of openness and communication in the home (+)

External Family Forces: positive (+) or negative (-)
1. Grandparents requiring more care (-)
2. Negative social forces and influence increasing for children (-)
3. Church youth group is struggling (-)
4. Parents' jobs are somewhat insecure (-)
5. Economy forcing major expense reductions (-)
6. Great network of friends (+)
7. Great church family (+)
8. Many siblings willing to help provide care for grandparents (+)
9. Grandparents are financially independent (+)
10. All family members live close by (+)

Once you have performed an environmental analysis for each of your leadership positions, you will want to take some time to analyze each of these forces and jot down some notes on Worksheet 2, Environmental Analysis, Part II (see p. 187) how internal and external forces are affecting your visions for the future. Think about how these forces are positively and negatively impacting your current leadership position. Draw some conclusions based on your analysis and write those down. Then, jot down some action items that relate to each of your conclusions.

Remember, you will not reach your potential for distinctive leadership in today's global marketplace if you do not understand the forces that shape your world. As King Solomon said, "It is not good to have zeal without knowledge"[9] and "the wisdom of the prudent is to give thought to their ways"[10] and "understanding is a fountain of life to those who have it."[11] A distinctive leader with the brand of God must be an active learner!

Walking Where Others Walk

A second method of understanding reality is to walk where others walk. God used this approach when he sent Jesus to earth to become human. Jesus worked like we work. He was tempted. He was hungry. He had been rich, yet he became poor for our sake. He knew what it was to be tired. He was afraid and fearful. He knew and knows what we go through. Thus, he understands our reality.

Joseph knew what it was like to manage Pharaoh's empire, but he also knew what it was like to be a slave and in prison. Moses knew the riches of Egypt in Pharaoh's household, yet he traded them to join his people who were being mistreated. Paul was among the most educated and wealthy, but he discovered a new reality on the road to Damascus. He considered all of his riches as rubbish in comparison to knowing Christ.[12]

As you attempt to define reality, you might want to do what Jesus and Joseph and Moses and Paul did: switch places. For example, you will get a better perspective of the current reality of your family by switching places with family members. If you are a parent, go spend some time in school with your children. Sit on the bus. Stand in line. Go to class. Sit where they sit. Eat where they eat. Meet their friends and see what they are like. Listen to what is going on around them. Attempt to see what they are facing each day. Live their schedule after school for a couple of days. Do their homework assignments and their chores at home.

You also might want to switch places with them at night. Sleep in their beds. While you are lying in their bed, let your mind wonder about the *view* from their bed. See if you can imagine what it's like to be a child in your home under your leadership. What do your children think about in their beds at night? What types of things do they worry about? Are they encouraged and strengthened and comforted by their environment? It is an interesting exercise that will help you understand where they are coming from. While you are completing these exercises, journal your thoughts, contemplate them, and share your observations with your children. Your perspective will help you grow!

At the office, too, switch places with some coworkers. If you are a senior executive or manager, go to work in the trenches with the people on your payroll. Flip burgers, wash cars, do laundry, answer the phone, work on the factory floor or out on the job site. You will gain new perspective, creating new building blocks for a foundation of great vision for your people. If you are a teacher, take the place of one of your students. If you are a doctor, become a patient. If you are an attorney, become a client. If you own an automobile dealership, go incognito and take your car in for service. These exercises may change your reality forever! Please use Worksheet 3, Walking Where Others Walk (page 188), to capture your insights.

Reading, Reading, Reading

A third way to understand and define reality is to read. It's been said that education is the architect of the mind and soul. Great business leaders, great governmental leaders, great parents, and great church leaders will all tell you to read! To be a distinctive leader, you must be well-read, informed, and have a voracious appetite for learning. Jesus was known to his peers as a carpenter but also as the one who taught with authority in the streets and in the synagogues.[13] Leaders are learners! Unfortunately, somewhere along the way, many of us lose our appetite for learning and tend to allow the forces of culture to shape who we are, what we know, and how we think. Remember, what you see determines who you will be!

We need to become a bit more like Curious George, asking questions, climbing ladders, testing things, tasting things, smelling things, and seeking an understanding of that which is around us. You should be reading a daily newspaper, reading books, checking the World Wide Web, and then choosing published material to inform you on subjects of interest that align with each of your sectors of life. If you're married, it is a good idea to read books together with your spouse. Doing so helps both of you focus on common themes and ideas that will be helpful to your marriage relationship. If you're single, invite a friend to share a book with you and meet at different times during the month to share thoughts and ideas.

My personal goals for reading change each year. Currently, I have a goal of reading two books every six months. It's a modest goal, but with responsibilities to my wife, three kids in school, three kids in sports, my mother, church, and job, it's still a handful. You can figure out reasonable reading goals that work for you.

Active Learning and Experience

A fourth way to learn is by experience. Most things in life simply cannot be fully appreciated until we experience them directly. I am sure I could learn some things about living in a developing nation from a book. However, I believe the learning experience would be richer and have more staying power if I visited and lived in a developing nation. This is why study abroad programs are so critical to higher education. Each of us needs to travel, see things, meet new people, and interact with this world like Jesus did.

Think about this: the places you visit, the things you experience, the people you meet, and the things you read will shape how you change over the next year. Make it a point to visit people, landmarks, museums, factories, financial districts, national parks, historic towns, local city council sessions, and different seats of government. These experiences will help shape your understanding of what things are like in a variety of sectors of life today.

As you define current reality, include others so they can be developing leaders with you. I have taken two separate strategic trips to Honduras with two of my three daughters. As daddy and daughter, we join a group of people doing medical missions and general labor in Choluteca, Honduras. These were transformational trips for us, exposing us to how much of the rest of the world lives. At times, when we weren't too exhausted to talk, we were able to discuss what we were experiencing and what we think the Christian responsibility is in light of what we saw—these were challenging conversations, forcing us to grapple together for answers. No book could impart the learning afforded by the trips. My children and I will never be the same.

Understanding Static Cling

"Do not pay attention to every word people say, or you may hear your servant cursing you—for you know in your heart that many times you yourself have cursed others."[14] These are wise words from Solomon. We all sin. As leaders we are faced with the reality of our limitations each and every day. One day my dear friend Tim was beginning a new leadership role on our campus, as director of admissions. As he drove to work, approaching the parking lot, the excitement grew for Tim. For him, it was the beginning of a role that would help shape his career and significantly affect the nature and strength of the university. At ten a.m., he would speak, for the first time as *boss*, to his professional staff. It was his first time to be "the leader" in this new capacity. As he placed the transmission of his vehicle in park and stepped out of his car, he noticed that his pants were loaded with *static cling*. He couldn't believe it! His legs looked like toothpicks. His body seemed to be drawing a little too much attention via the static cling.

How could this happen? *Of all times*, he thought. *This looks horrible. How can I lead with static cling in my pants?*

Spiritual static cling is a real phenomenon for all of us, revealing things we really don't want others to see. It causes us to look funny and appear less qualified to lead. Well, Moses had a little static cling of his own. First of all, his identity was twisted. He was abandoned. His own mother placed him in a makeshift boat—a basket coated with pitch and tar—and launched him into the Nile River on his own. Thus, he grew up as a Hebrew in Pharaoh's court without his own mother. He was a murderer, having single-handedly killed an Egyptian in the streets for beating a Hebrew. And he was a coward. He ran away to Midian because he was afraid of the people and Pharaoh, and he was anxious when God asked him to go visit Pharaoh alone. He continually asked the Lord, "Who will go with me?" He explained to the Lord that this call to leadership with distinction was really fine, but he, himself, had never really been eloquent, neither in the past nor since God had been speaking to him. In fact, Moses said to the Lord, "I am slow of speech and tongue."[15] In other words, you probably better get someone else for the job! Moses incessantly pleaded with God to have someone else lead. This angered the Lord and the Scripture says that the Lord's anger burned against Moses.[16]

Phenomenally, with all his static cling, God was able to transform this ordinary sinful man, Moses, into an extraordinary leader for the Israelites and an exceptional model of leadership for you and me today.

Feedback: The Breakfast of Champions

There is a sixth way of understanding reality: get feedback from others and take time for personal reflection. King Solomon said, "He who listens to a life-giving rebuke will be at home with the wise."[17]

Great leaders accept criticism and advice. Generally, friends who care enough to share are, indeed, friends that last. Criticism usually stings at the time, but it often becomes a blessing for a lifetime, as it accounts for much of the progress in a person or an organization. Like an Olympian, a leader must expect and plan for pain. According to Bob Richards, an Olympic gold medalist, winners of the gold all have a specific plan for handling the pain. "You never win the gold without hurting," said Bob.[18]

One of my colleagues compiled, in paragraph form, some of Solomon's wisdom, specifically related to accepting criticism:

> It is a badge of honor to accept valid criticism. If you refuse criticism, you will end in poverty and disgrace; if you accept criticism, you are on the road to fame. Proud men end in shame, but the meek become wise. Anyone willing to be corrected is on the pathway to life. Anyone refusing has lost his chance. Don't refuse to accept criticism; get all the help you can. A fool thinks he needs no advice, but a wise man listens to others. To learn, you must want to be taught. To refuse reproof is stupid. Though good advice lies deep within a counselor's heart, the wise man will draw it out. The advice of a wise man refreshes like water from a mountain spring. Those accepting it become aware of the pitfalls on ahead. A man who refuses to admit his mistakes can never be successful. But if he confesses and forsakes them, he gets another chance. The good man asks advice from friends; the wicked plunge ahead and fall. Wounds from a friend are better than kisses from an enemy. Don't go ahead with your plans without accepting the advice of others. Get all the advice you can and be wise the rest of your life. Friendly suggestions are as pleasant as perfume.[19]

To build a brand of leadership that matters, each of us needs to know how we are perceived by others. We need to take a good look in the mirror and understand the reality of our own strengths and weaknesses. Worksheet 4, A Look in the Mirror, is designed to help you perform a 360-degree assessment similar to those used by many organizations today. The worksheet is simple and focuses on behaviors. It asks people to tell you what behaviors they would like to see more of, what behaviors they would like to see less of, and what behaviors they want you to definitely continue. Select a few key positions from Worksheet 1 for which you believe a 360-degree procedure would be helpful to you and your leadership. Then, distribute copies of Worksheet 4 (page 189) to at least three colleagues, three subordinates, and two people who hold a position of supervision over you. For example, if you want to "look in the mirror" as father, distribute the worksheet to three of your friends who know you and your family, a couple of your siblings, your spouse, your children, and your parents and/or grandparents.

Once you receive the feedback forms, find a quiet place and take some time to review them carefully, making notes as you think about the comments you received. As you reflect on the comments provided, you may move through stages of emotion that can be remembered through the acronym, S-A-R-A-H. You may feel Shock, Anger, and Resentment. If you do, you must take time to process your feelings and then make sure to move through to the stages of Acceptance and Hope.

Hopefully, you will be an "alchemist" during this review process, a rare individual who is adept at transforming the base minerals of low-quality feedback into pure gold. An alchemist's behavior follows a few patterns that we can learn from. Table 6.2 exhibits the work of an alchemist in comparison to a normal leader.[20]

TABLE 6.2 The Philosopher's Stone (from Fernando Bartolome and John Weeks, "Find the Gold in Toxic Feedback," *Harvard Business Review* (April 2007), 24.		
When Feedback is:	**Most Managers:**	**But Alchemists:**
Personally Offensive	Allow anger and defensiveness to cloud their understanding	Listen carefully to the message while managing their emotions
	Provide explanations, which speakers usually dismiss as excuses	Don't immediately try to explain their actions
	Allow the emotional tone to escalate	Maintain a neutral tone
Inaccurate	Reflexively question the feedback's accuracy	Postpone accuracy considerations until later
	Focus on the feedback's inaccuracies	Focus on the accuracies
	React to the literal meaning	Look beyond the literal meaning to learn about people's perceptions, assumptions, and attitudes
Irrelevant	Focus on all of the feedback, pertinent or not	Focus on just the information that can help them deal with the problems they face
Unbalanced	Lose touch with their own strengths and so remain vulnerable to obsessing about their weaknesses	Place negative feedback in the context of prior positive feedback from others, as well as generate their own internal positive feedback messages

Next, use Worksheet 5, A Look in the Mirror: Conclusions and Action Items, to move toward an action plan based on your Look in the Mirror test. Record the following:

1. Top three areas in which you would like to improve
2. Reasons why you want to improve in these areas
3. Action plans you must put in place to improve

As you engage this process, be aware that the people you've selected provide these comments with some level of risk, which they have taken because they want to invest in your personal growth and development as a leader. Do not give rebuttals or seek more specific ratings, and don't share your results with everyone. Instead, thank participants for their involvement with you and seek clarification on any comments you don't fully understand.

Reflecting on Your Past

Another exercise that will help you understand your own reality is to create what Dr. Noel Tichy calls a personal *Journey Line*.[21] A Journey Line is a graphic of the high points and low points in your leadership journey, noting emotional energy, values, and ideas that shaped those particular peaks and troughs.

You can use Worksheet 6, Journey Line, to plot your own personal Journey. When you complete it, share it with someone or a group you lead. The exercise will do two things. First, it will help you better understand the formative elements of your leadership life to date. Second, it will draw your colleagues in to your life, helping them understand who you are and why you have a passion for the things you do. It is another way to uncover a piece of the reality puzzle.

For several years, I have been administering Journey Line exercises to students who attend our college's annual Leadership Summit in Colorado and to men at various leadership gatherings across the country. Attendees post their completed Journey Lines on the walls for all to see. Examining these public portraits of life is a humbling experience for all who participate. The process reveals what is constructing our reality.

The data from this year's Leadership Summit showed there are six major areas of life that construct our reality, ranked by their amount of influence:

1. Life with family and friends (25%)
2. Life growing up (23 %)

3. School life/work life (21%)
4. Spiritual life (17%)
5. Love life (7%)
6. Life struggles and temptations (7%)

I will provide one last way to understand individual and group reality: poetry writing. Yes, I'm serious. Based on Beverly Daniel Tatum's poem "I am from," the poem you write will tell you many things about yourself that help you understand your leadership reality and the realities of those you are leading. The poem has four stanzas:

Stanza 1	This stanza begins, "I am from . . ." and then you list familiar items found around your home either growing up or now.
Stanza 2	This stanza begins, "I am from . . ." and then you list familiar foods prepared or eaten around your home.
Stanza 3	This stanza begins, "I am from . . ." and then you note family sayings that were a part of your upbringing and often heard in your home.
Stanza 4	This stanza begins, "I am from . . ." and then you list the people in your family and/or your home growing up.

List all of your items, food, sayings, and family members in each of the stanzas. Then, analyze why those were so real for you and what meaning they create in your current life. Also, if you are attempting to do some team building, this exercise offers a great opportunity to bring people together through shared stories and explanations. Try it with your immediate family!

Pray, Pray, Pray

Finally, pray, pray, pray. C. S. Lewis wrote eloquently about the nature of prayer:

Can we believe that God ever really modifies His action in response to the suggestions of men? For infinite wisdom does not need telling what is best, and infinite goodness needs no urging to do it.

But neither does God need any of those things that are done by finite agents, whether living or inanimate. He could, if He chose, repair our bodies miraculously without food; or give us food without the aid of farmers, bakers and butchers; or knowledge without the aid of learned men; or convert the heathen without missionaries.

Instead, He allows soils and weather and animals and the muscles, minds and wills of men to cooperate with the execution of His will . . . It is not really stranger, nor less strange, that my prayers should affect the course of events than my other actions should do so. They have not advised or changed God's mind—that is, His overall purpose. But that purpose will be realized in different ways according to the actions, including the prayers, of His creatures.[22]

The thoughts of C. S. Lewis underscore that we have the authority and privilege of cooperating, through prayer, in the will of God. From my perspective, prayer does at least five things for the believer seeking to create a life of distinction.

1. **Prayer brings you into God's presence.** Through prayer you engage in deep conversation with God. You talk and listen. His purposes, presence, and power are made known through times of reflection and prayer.[23]

2. **Prayer focuses your attention and reveals your priorities.** It forces you to articulate thoughts, ideas, and desires to God. An examination of one's prayer life is much like examining one's checkbook. It reveals much about what is important and exhibits the deep desires of the heart and mind.[24]

3. **Prayer keeps you from falling into temptation.** Jesus prayed often that God would keep him from falling into Satan's schemes. He also admonished the disciples to pray so they would not fall into temptation.[25]

4. **Prayer helps you get things done.** We are told that the faithful and fervent prayer of a righteous man does much. We pray for goals, for people, for nations, for protection, and for God's will to be done in our lives.[26]

5. **Prayer grants insight and vision.** Paul prayed often that the eyes of our hearts might be opened. He prayed for wisdom, knowledge, depth of insight, and for the mystery of Christ to be revealed to us. Jesus prayed that the Holy Spirit would take from what he knew and make it known to all of us.[27]

Key Points

1. One can observe a lot by watching.
2. Each of us lives in unique towers, influencing us to misunderstand, or at least not fully understand, the current reality around us.
3. Each of us has biases stemming from our own myopic tower dwelling.
4. Confronting and understanding reality is essential to good visions.
5. Climbing new towers, walking where others walk, experiencing new things, acknowledging static cling, getting feedback, reading, and praying are the building blocks of understanding our current realities.
6. From current research, we know that family life, school and work life, growing up life, romantic life, spiritual life, and worldly struggles comprise our most poignant reality.
7. Good eyes see the unseen and perceive that which is eternal.[28]

Challenge

Jesus often hit the Pharisees right between the eyes. Their inability to accurately perceive reality was one of his main areas of focus. On one occasion he said to them,

> Woe to you, blind guides! You say, "If anyone swears by the temple, it means nothing; but if anyone swears by the gold of the temple, he is bound by his oath." You blind fools! Which is greater: the gold, or the temple that makes the gold sacred? You also say, "If anyone swears by the altar, it means nothing; but if anyone swears by the gift on it, he is bound by his oath." You blind men! Which is greater: the gift, or the altar that makes the gift sacred? Therefore, he who swears by the altar swears by it and by everything on it.
>
> And he who swears by the temple swears by it and by the one who dwells in it. And he who swears by heaven swears by God's throne and by the one who sits on it. Woe to you, teachers of the law and Pharisees, you hypocrites! You give a tenth of your spices—mint, dill and cummin. But you have neglected the more important matters of the law—justice, mercy and faithfulness. You should have practiced the latter, without neglecting the former. You blind guides! You strain out a gnat but swallow a camel.[29]

Jesus is holding nothing back here. He tells these religious leaders they are wicked because they do not see things as they should. This critical rebuke by Jesus offers a challenge to us, as well. Are you seeing his reality? Do you understand the real spiritual battle that is taking place? How is your understanding of reality impacting your ability to find big ideas?

Exploring Big Ideas

1. Describe your tower. What are some of its distinguishing elements?

2. What contributes to cave dwelling for so many?

3. What approaches work best to help you get out of your tower and understand your reality?

4. How did Jesus stay in touch with his reality? Did he do anything to foster and nurture his perception?

5. How did Jesus' ability to perceive the hearts and minds of people and the spiritual battle around him contribute to his leadership success? List examples where his perceptive nature resulted in distinctive leadership.

6. How did your Journey Line reveal your reality?

7. In Matthew 6:22, what did Jesus mean by saying, "The eye is the lamp of the body"?

Chapter Seven

DRAFTING THE BLUEPRINT

For I know the plans I have for you, declares the LORD,
plans to prosper you and not to harm you,
plans to give you hope and a future.
Then you will call upon me and come and pray to me,
and I will listen to you. You will seek me and find me
when you seek me with all your heart.

—JEREMIAH 29:11–12

D r. Horace Williams, professor of philosophy at the University of North Carolina in the early twentieth century, walked into his classroom one day. As one of his students recounted,

> He walked to the window, where he stood with folded arms and gazed out silently at a dogwood tree. Minutes passed. Had he forgotten us?
>
> "Tell me, Mr. Richardson," he finally said in a slow drawl, "What is the most important part of an ox cart?"
>
> There were thirty of us in the class. He already knew all our names. Jack Richardson thought for a moment, then replied, "I should say an oxen, sir."
>
> "Wrong. Mr. Ross?"
>
> "The wheel, professor?" I volunteered.
>
> "Wrong. Mr. Nelson?" Nelson also was wrong.
>
> Six more students gave wrong answers, and finally professor Williams turned to face us for the first time.

"No, gentlemen, it's the concept of a cart, the blueprint. After the blueprint has been made, any jackleg can do the rest. The blueprint lasts forever."[1]

———

The blueprint we draft to guide our life will determine how we live and lead.

What about your blueprint? Is your current blueprint branded by God? Does it matter? Is it big? Is it distinctive? Is it powerful? Is it legendary? Is it leading you, your family, or your business to a meaningful destination?

Planning is only important *if* you believe the future is important! The Lord of Heaven has plans for you and me, plans to prosper us, not harm us. The pattern is consistent throughout the pages of the sacred text.

The cross was planned. While we were yet sinners, Christ died for us, the righteous for the unrighteous. God has an ongoing plan, too, and is preparing for our future. You are not the product of randomness. Even if you were an accident to "someone," you are not an accident to God. His plans, purpose, and his preparation include you. They always have.

When it came to planning, Jesus was a master. He left nothing to chance. His timing was perfect. Sometimes he helped immediately, as in the case of the centurion's servant. Other times he delayed, as in the case of Lazarus or his trip to Jerusalem. His decision-making was based on his overall plan.

Even Satan knew there was a plan. He simply had a difficult time knowing what it was: "Once, when Jesus arrived in the region of the Gadarenes, two-demon possessed men coming from the tombs met him. They were so violent that no one could pass that way. 'What do you want with us, Son of God?' they shouted. 'Have you come here to torture us before the appointed time?'"[2] The demons knew Jesus had a plan and attempted to challenge his plan and his timing.

Every time Jesus' enemies tried to back him into a corner, Jesus asked questions or somehow eluded their grasp because he was prepared. When he resisted the temptations of Satan in the desert through a precise knowledge of the Old Testament, it was no accident. Jesus had studied the text well in advance. He knew what God's word said and how to apply it in his real life. Indeed, he endured the suffering of the cross because he planned for it and was ready. His life and connection with God prepared him.

So, the obvious question is this: If planning and purpose are part of God's nature, don't you believe it should be part of yours?

Leaders are ultimately responsible for planning the future. Only God holds the future, but we're still called to plan. Jack Welch at GE said a top priority for leaders is to "control your destiny or someone else will." He asked leaders at GE to decide where they were taking the company. "Leaders shouldn't manage," he said, "they should lead." Visionary leaders should be crafting a vision of the future and communicating the vision in a way that compels others to want to fulfill it.

Jesus modeled the principle. He sent out "twelve" with a clear purpose and plan. He explained their target market (Jews). He gave a specific message to preach (the kingdom of God is near). He provided instructions on what to do, what to take, and how to deal with people, and he warned the disciples of the dangers inherent to the mission.

Jesus might ask you, "Where are you taking your life?" What plans and purposes are in your future? Where are you taking your family? Where are you taking your business? Where are you taking the church? Meaningful answers to these questions come only when you engage in purposeful soul-searching regarding the life and purposes you have been given.

When you understand your current reality, it is time to begin crafting a vision, establishing specific leadership goals, and creating a plan of action for each of your divine appointments. In essence, you must chart the course.

Many models exist to help undertake this type of work. However, vision is more art than science and the results are ultimately up to the unique touch of the craftsman. In this section, I provide you with a few tools intended to help you capture and craft the "big ideas" that will guide your vision for each of your divine appointments.

Table 7.1 identifies five basic elements that are essential to developing a distinctive vision. They are not necessarily listed in order of progression and sequence. Rather, these elements are interrelated and bind themselves together naturally, so you can complete them in any order that works for you.

| **TABLE 7.1** |
| Essential Vision & Planning Elements |
| 1. Vision and Mission Statements |
| 2. Plans of Action: Positions, Goals, Tactics, Assessment |
| 3. How Others Can Help Develop Your Mission |
| 4. Developing a Teachable Point of View (TPOV): Ideas and Values |
| 5. Benchmarking |

Vision and Mission Statements

Many people are confused over the difference between a vision and a mission statement. The difference is one of degree. A vision statement is typically broad and inspirational. It does not include much detail, but focusing instead on painting a large picture using broad brush strokes to portray the future. For example, the vision of Abilene Christian University is "to educate students for Christian service and leadership throughout the world." This short sentence is repeated often on campus and paints a broad understanding of what we are there to do. In the College of Business Administration, we adapted the university vision with one small change as our own, "to educate *business* students for Christian service and leadership throughout the world."

However, our mission statement is much more detailed. You will notice that the mission describes our ultimate purpose (to glorify God) and then offers specifics about how we intend to accomplish our goals. It describes our mission in the context of our vision:

> The Mission of the College of Business Administration is to glorify God by creating a distinctively Christian environment in which excellent teaching, combined with scholarship, promotes the intellectual, personal, and spiritual growth of business students, and educates them for Christian service and leadership throughout the world.

I suggest you develop a mission statement that articulates and explains the fundamental purpose of each of your positions. A good mission statement identifies who you are (whether that "you" is an organization or an individual), your fundamental reason for existence (describing your current divine appointments), the intended scope of your operations (world, industry, neighborhood, school, family, etc.), what you hope to accomplish, and the ideas and principles that will guide your future. You should find that your values and principles overlap the various positions you hold, but the specific mission in each of these positions should be somewhat different. You may want to use Worksheet 7, Mission Statement Development (page 192), to guide your work.

Through my own research with church leaders, I discovered that few people put an emphasis on leadership in their homes and churches. Only twenty-five percent of church leaders indicate that they have a family mission statement at all. Of those, only six percent indicate it is written and understood. Contrast these percentages to the global marketplace, where every business leader knows the importance of a mission statement, articulating why the business is organized, where it is headed, and what principles will guide the journey. Evidently, this message is not penetrating the domains of home and church.

More than fifty percent of the families created by marriage end in divorce. Shouldn't it matter more to have a clearly articulated purpose for the family than for a business? Shouldn't we invest some time to contemplate and communicate the important ideas that will guide and shape the destiny of our families?

God told Israel to make the family mission statement clearly understood by everyone in the family: "Impress [the commandments] on your children. Talk about them when you sit at home and when you walk along the road, when you lie down and when you get up. Tie them as symbols on your hands and bind them on your foreheads. Write them on the doorframes of your houses and on your gates."[3] If we don't do the same, we will share the predicament of Alice in Wonderland: "Sir, Cheshire Puss, Alice began. Where ought I go from here? That depends upon where you want to get to, said the cat. But I don't really know, said Alice. Then it doesn't much matter, said the cat."[4]

Are you taking time to *sit at home* and *walk along the road* with your family members? I often joke with Jeanne, saying we should sell our home and buy a motor home because it seems we are always on the go, rarely spending time at home. I bet, on average, I spend less than a couple of hours a week sitting at home, excluding meals. When was the last time your family took a walk and talked about things along the road? Without planning and purpose, such activities won't happen.

Several years ago, I decided to craft a family mission statement. It took nearly six months for me to do it. It was something I wanted to do. It was good for me to struggle and contemplate what I would put on one page for my family to see. I read and read numerous scriptures, books, and old sermon notes of mine. I listened to old cassette tapes I had on file. I scribbled and I scratched. I thought about what was really important in life and what I wanted to communicate to our girls. I thought a lot about why God gave me a family in the first place. You see, we experienced three miscarriages early in our marriage. One included losing twins. These intimate tragedies caused me to ponder greatly the meaning of this family I now had.

Our family mission statement is reproduced in Appendix B (page 197) for you to see, as one example of how you might approach your own.

Plans of Action

Once your personal mission statement is complete, you'll need to draft a written plan to help you achieve your vision. For each position of leadership you identified as a top priority, you need to develop goals and objectives. I am not a big fan of complicated planning, but I am in favor of written plans because they are developed out of time, purpose, and passion. President Theodore Roosevelt said it well when he argued the actual plan itself is not so important, but the process of planning is. Most businesses have three-year plans, one-year plans, and a series of monthly targets and objectives that are reviewed continuously. However, again, few families or churches have such planning documents.

Using Worksheet 8, Overall Goals and Objectives (page 193), write out three to five specific goals for each leadership position you identified as a top priority. These goals should relate directly to your work in defining your current reality. Again, this exercise will take some time and thoughtful reflection on your part. As Stephen Covey has suggested for decades, begin with the end in mind. For your family goals, you may want to use Luke 2:52 ("And Jesus grew in wisdom and stature, and in favor with God and men.") as a categorical framework: spiritual, intellectual, social, and physical.

You may also enjoy engaging in what I call *mega goal setting*. One of my mentors and friends, James R. Porter, a successful entrepreneur and Christian business man, suggests that individuals annually engage in an omnibus approach to goal setting, listing in ten minutes as many goals as you can, to be accomplished over a two-year period. The list may be as long as twenty, thirty, or even fifty goals. Once the list is complete, you analyze, distill, and categorize each goal with prioritization. You may then keep these goals and your worksheet before you throughout the year as a planning tool. At the end of each year, perform an annual audit of your progress. Then recalibrate, and shoot for more.

In our family, to be sure, we don't hit all goals each year. But, I will tell you, I am amazed at what we have accomplished because we have a living, breathing plan that is important and embraced by the entire family.

The document is reviewed several times per year and is updated each fall during our annual family planning retreat. Each fall, I schedule a weekend for the entire family to go away somewhere and spend two nights at a remote location. The focus of our time is family fun and planning. An easel, markers, popcorn, notebooks, select movies, and copies of the family plan are used during our time together. Don't laugh now. I actually put together an agenda for the weekend.

Our overriding question for the retreat each year is this: If anything were possible, what would our family be like?

We engage in two or three short planning sessions and complete our agenda, answering our questions and beginning to formulate our new family plan. There are three primary objectives for our retreat. First, we want to review our plan as a family, providing an opportunity for all members of the family to have input on how we did during the past year. Second, we want to update and refresh our objectives for the next three to five years. We all take ownership in our plan. And we also use that retreat to have lots and lots of fun: shopping, go-karts, bowling, hiking, bicycling, movies, games, and just talking and hugging fill the rest of our agenda.

How Others Can Help Develop Your Mission

The importance of having a personal mentor became clearer to me a few years ago when I was painting a room in our home. In typical fashion, it took me longer to paint this particular room than I had planned! I seem unable to paint any room in one day. Thus, to my wife's dismay, the room is usually out of order for days on end while I attempt to find the time and the discipline to get the job done. One evening in the midst of my struggle, our daughter Michelle (ten years old at the time) asked if she could help me paint. She had never painted a room in our home before, nor had she ever asked to, so the request caught me off guard.

I hesitated, not wanting her to disrupt my pace or somehow devalue my splendid work. When I came to my senses, I said, "Sure, honey. I would love to have you help me paint." My first approach was to lecture her about how to paint. I spoke about the way you protect the carpet and couches with covers. I talked to her about the importance of good ventilation. We had some discussion about the importance of having the proper amount of paint on the brush, stressing that it was critical to good coverage on the wall. I even explained how to stroke the brush on the wall back and forth to utilize both sides of the brush for more efficient painting.

She diligently listened to all this, then grabbed the brush and began to paint by herself. I watched with angst as she attempted to paint. At that moment, I knew my teaching method had failed to educate her sufficiently for the task at hand. She was floundering until I modeled the way for her, taking her hand in mine while we painted. Hand in hand, she learned to hold the brush, dip the paint, and stroke the brush on the wall.

In that situation, there was no replacement for someone taking the time to personally model the way. It's the same in so many areas of life, isn't it? We can all think back on times when we were the beneficiaries of an individual who took the time to mentor and model the way for us! We all need a little help from someone now and then, especially regarding eternal issues of life and leadership. Find a mentor to help. We are all limited!

My grandfather, Harvey Borchert, was a great influence on me. Working together many weekends, he taught me about marriage, humility, servant-leadership, tree trimming, painting, yard work, laughter, and simple faith. He was there when I was baptized. Indeed, he was a primary reason I came to believe and be baptized. Message to grandparents: you have a major role to play in shaping the lives of young people. Continue building a brand of leadership that matters with those around you until the Lord takes your breath away! Message to parents: put your children in the presence of grandparents, for they will be forever changed in their presence.

Will Ed Warren and Vernon Boyd were my preachers growing up. They, along with many sweet lady Bible class teachers, implanted the word of God and an opportunity for the Spirit of Christ to form within me.

Silas and Edna Mae Shotwell and Steve and Jane Watson gave us big ideas regarding the fundamentals of grace and discipleship. Silas shared deep treasures from God's word revealed to us like never before. We longed, each Sunday and Wednesday evening, to hear his insight and his proclamation of God's saving grace. Steve and Jane showed us a model of lifestyle evangelism that changed our paradigm of what the church is ultimately about: bringing people to Jesus!

From a family perspective, Jack and Ann Griggs have allowed us to adopt and adapt many big ideas. For example, Jack and Ann showed us the power of teaching our three daughters to be best friends from an early age. They opened up to us the idea of "Lytle Power," teaching our children to call upon one another if they are in distress by yelling "LYTLE POWER" with maximum vocal capacity. When our daughters were small and would broadcast this call, every Lytle girl responded in emergency fashion, coming to the aid of their best friends, their sisters. We believe this bond will be important for them long after Jeanne and I are gone.

We also learned a travel game from Jack that was special to our family when the kids were little. At one time, Jack told me this game could be the best single financial investment I make in the children's university educations. I did not understand, but I listened. We called it "Who Wants to Be a Great Student?" The game is played with simple rules. First, once the trip begins, all children are responsible for buying their own meals. Second, the only way to earn money to buy the meals is to answer rounds and rounds of test questions successfully. The game has categories like Bible, Science, Math, Weather, Spelling, and Vocabulary. Jeanne and I administered the game and awarded points for correct answers. Each child was able to collect $.05 for each correct answer. If someone answers incorrectly, the next child can answer correctly for $.10. We played as long as the kids wanted to play and eat!

I must admit that it did backfire a bit when we first tried this on a trip to Colorado. The kids were fairly young and had each earned more than $3.00 that day. We stopped to eat. They each told us they were not hungry. Once we were back on the road, Jeanne and I ate our meals while they watched with sad eyes. In reality, they were hungry but didn't want to use their money on food. Consequently, they mooched off of us and devoured all of our snacks on the first day—ha! Then Hannah explained how difficult it was to spend her money because each dollar was precious to her. "Trust me," I told her. "I know! Each dollar is precious to me too!"

Though it backfired a bit at first, the game provided a fun opportunity over the years for PSAT and SAT/ACT preparation. Jack was right: it has been a great investment in their college education.

It is the responsibility of one generation to pass on truth to the next. However, we must be willing to seek and find these treasures. No doubt, my life is better today because of the ideas many along the path have shared with me. They have helped me become distinctive, seeing things I never could see before in my professional life, my family life, and my social life.

Developing a Teachable Point of View

The distinctive leader's vision must not only be compelling and involve big ideas; it must also be teachable. Dr. Tichy writes, "A teachable point of view is a cohesive set of ideas and concepts that a person is able to articulate clearly to others. The difference between an excellent solo player and world-class leader is the ability to teach others."[5]

Jeff Immelt, General Electric CEO, frames his vision of leadership around three teachable ideas. First, leaders drive change. Second, leaders develop other leaders. Third, leaders give back.

David Novak, former CEO of YUM brands (Pizza Hut, Kentucky Fried Chicken, Taco Bell, Long John Silver's), built the YUM Dynasty around his belief that the soft stuff drives the hard numbers. To build the dynasty, he espoused this:

1. Managers must cast the right shadow of leadership.
2. People must know what goals lead to improved performance.
3. People must feel appreciated and recognized.[6]

In order to help you capture and articulate your own vision in a teachable way, you can engage in the following exercises.

Exercise One. Close your eyes and imagine your ideal day at work. Use Worksheet 9, My Ideal Day (page 194), to record your answers. Please don't let your left-brain dominate this exercise. Don't create a list of technical things you would like to get done. Rather, work on breakthrough thoughts and ideas. Imagine a video camera following you— what would an ideal day look like for you, your family, your church, or your organization? Where would your office be located? What would the office complex look like? What would the interior look like? Who would be working with you? What types of interactions would occur? What would the results of a good day be for you? This exercise reveals what you enjoy doing and what you see as important in your life, part of your teachable point of view.

Exercise Two. Now imagine what an ideal two years at work or at church or at home looks like. Use Worksheet 10, Looking Back: A Two-Year Review (page 195), to record a story you write. Pretend you are a reporter for a periodical like the *Wall Street Journal* or *Time* or *Vogue* or *Better Homes and Gardens* or *Christianity Today* or *USA Today*—whatever you like to read—and write a retrospective piece on what you, as leader, will have accomplished in the next two years. If you discipline yourself, you should be able to write this story in about an hour. It will be difficult, but once you have written the story, share it with a friend and see if that person can help you discern what big ideas are embedded in your story. Can someone else summarize your point of view? How can you make your vision more teachable for others?

Exercise Three. Now, review your notes from the first two exercises as you prepare a speech for your colleagues. Write an outline for a five-minute speech that articulates your teachable point of view. Have someone video record your speech. Once your record your speech, have several friends review the speech and provide coaching to help you bring out your teachable point of view.

In order for these exercises to be helpful, you must take them seriously and force yourself to move out of your comfort zone into writing and speech-making, two key practices in ensuring that your vision is teachable.[7]

Benchmarking

Another approach to vision casting is to benchmark your ideas against those in great speeches by great leaders. Great speeches usually have three fundamental elements. First, they will describe the current reality and the need for change. Second, they will describe a general direction and dream for the future. Finally, they will tell how to get there. In other words, an effective speech renders the future for all who listen.

In his famous "I Have a Dream" speech, Martin Luther King, Jr., creates a beautiful tapestry of symbols, language, and metaphors that describe his view of the past, the current reality, and the future. Dr. King had a simple and strong teachable point of view. His speech can be broken down and analyzed as follows:

1. View of the Past—A Promissory Note. We have great opportunity in this land but one hundred years after the signing of the Emancipation Proclamation, the American black people are still not free.

2. View of Present—A Broken Promise. The promise of equal opportunity for all people was broken for the black community.

3. View of Future—A Dream. In the future, racial hatred and social injustice can give way to true equality and community among all people.

Each time I listen to King's speech, I am amazed at how he crafted such a powerful three-point vision using ideas and imagery that stir all but the coldest of hearts to action. Moving through the failures of the past and the brokenness of the present into the hope of the future, King finally invites all his listeners to join hands and declare those joyous words: "Free at last! Free at last! Thank God almighty, we are free at last!"

In closing this chapter, remember that distinctive visions always begin with a time of position identification and prioritization, determining what positions you hold that are of utmost importance to you. Then a time of reflection and soul-searching must begin. Where do you come from? Why are you here? What big ideas guide you? Where are you taking those entrusted to you? How will you navigate the journey? Once you engage the struggle and cast a vision, your work will result in a recognizable passion for achieving the vision.

When I set out to cast a vision, I reflect on God's love and presence (Matt. 22:37; Ps. 46:10) and remember who I am in relation to God and others (Phil. 2:5–8; Mic. 6:8). I pray for a sharp vision of God's brand (Eph. 1:18) and for the power and influence to make that brand known to the world.

Now that your perspectives and positions are in focus, it is time to connect to the power grid that will enable you to supply energy and switch your plans into action on a daily basis. Let's power in, power on, and power up!

Key Points

1. Much energy is required for a meaningful plan to be born and launched into operation. It only works if the process is purposeful and attended to.
2. Your mission statement should address who you are, why you are here, what you plan to do, and where you will do your work. It may also address some elements of achievement.
3. Your plan should reflect BIG IDEAS and BIG DREAMS.
4. Your plan should reflect the promises of almighty God.
5. Your goals should be specific, measurable, and achievable.
6. Your plan should be teachable.
7. Your completed plans should be monitored, measured, and updated annually.

Challenge

I often wonder why Hollywood is so powerful. Why is it that a relatively small band of artists, whose lives are usually far from exemplary, become such powerful role models for our culture? These people impact our values, our language, our dress, and our lifestyles in extraordinary ways. One simple reason is that people are watching them. Once they become the focus of attention, they become influential.

Our challenge is to bring appropriate role models and mentors into our lives and the lives of those important to us. Homes, churches, and businesses need to develop spiritual visions of greatness with our eyes fixed on Jesus and on other good people. We need to capture ideas that promote distinctive leadership and offer joy. I encourage you to find mentors to aid you as you craft visions of greatness. By watching those you truly admire, you shape who you will become.

Exploring Big Ideas

1. Describe a person or family who plans. What can you learn?

2. Describe why you think planning is so difficult for so many.

3. What factors do you think contribute most to successful planning?

4. What factors contribute to its demise? Why do you think this is so?

5. List some things that can be done to ensure the development of strong, Christ-centered plans for you and your family. Share with others if present.

6. What is so powerful about Martin Luther King's "I Have a Dream" speech?

7. How did Martin Luther King paint a picture of reality AND hope?

Part Three

——————

POWER

Chapter Eight

POWER IN

*Do not be afraid or discouraged because of the king of Assyria
and the vast army with him, for there is a greater power with us than with him.*
—2 CHRONICLES 32:7

*I am going to send you what my Father has promised;
but stay in the city until you have been clothed with power from on high.*
—MARK 24:49

Vaclav Havel had big ideas but no powerful guns and weapons of war. His power was in the force of his life and ideals. This big idea was quite distinctive from the Marxist Czech philosophers of his day, who assumed the only way to overthrow the Communist government was through armed revolution. Quite to the contrary, with Havel's distinctive leadership, in his own words, "Communism was overthrown by life, by thought, by human dignity."[1]

Havel was a dreamer and impassioned visionary. Even while living under the crushing weight of Communism in the late twentieth century, Havel dreamed of great things for his country. Embedded in Havel's ideas is a belief in the inextricability of morality and politics, and his commitment to this relationship spurred a revolutionary overthrow of a corrupt system. Havel often said, "The real test of a man is not when he plays the role that he wants for himself, but when he plays the role destiny has for him."

"The world might actually be changed by the force of truth," Havel also said, "the power of a truthful word, the strength of a free spirit, conscience, and responsibility—with no guns, no lust for power, no political wheeling and dealing."[2] Havel's positive mark on humanity will long be viewed as one of the greatest of all time.

Havel was not conflicted about power. Power and influence could be used as a force that crippled mighty armies and political citadels and replaced them with responsible and moral leadership. Many people are ambivalent or uncomfortable with power, but to be a serious leader, one must understand that power is real and that it underpins leadership for good or bad.

When quizzing our daughter Hannah years ago, I asked, "Hannah, are you powerful?" She said, "Yes." I asked, "Why do you say so?" She responded, "God is power and God lives in me." Precisely, my dear!

Unfortunately, many people are not as comfortable as Hannah with the idea of power. Plenty of good people feel insecure or presumptuous in thinking about their own power. Discussions often treat power as synonymous with evil, and in such a context admitting an interest in power is the same as conceding a moral failing.[3] Often, we accept that Lord Acton had it completely right: power corrupts and absolute power corrupts absolutely, no exceptions. Yet logically, most people would agree they don't want their children to lead weak, helpless lives incapable of any greatness. Whether we acknowledge it or not, power is central to leadership and forms the foundations and structures of government, sociology, psychology, history, and religion—and that power is not essentially good or bad.[4]

John Gardner cautions, "Power is not to be confused with status or prestige. It is the capacity to ensure the outcomes one wishes and to prevent those one does not wish. Power as we are now speaking of it—power in the social dimension—is simply the capacity to bring about certain intended consequences in the behavior of others."[5]

Whatever your view of power, I submit that without it, you will never build a brand of leadership that matters in the lives of those you love and lead. Think about it. Who desires to work for a boss categorized as powerless? How many of you clamor to belong to a church classified as weak? How many of you are thankful for feeble leadership in your home? How many citizens would stand up and be counted for their desire to live in a city, state, or nation where leadership was unstable? Most of us want to be guided and guarded by powerful leaders.

The problem is not with power. The problem is that many of us don't comprehend that power is not ours but God's, on loan to us to accomplish God's purposes. Because of this misunderstanding, Christians too often think of power as something they should stay away from. People equate meekness with weakness and humility with vulnerability. To be sweet and kind is to be soft and yielding. The view out of this tower sees Jesus weeping and washing feet—an incredible mark of his leadership. Unfortunately, this view fails to see Jesus also standing up to authorities across religious, political, and social boundaries. Jesus, without hesitation, directly confronted Satan.

I tell you the truth, Jesus entered our world in power. He was gifted with the Holy Spirit of God.[6] His purpose was aligned with his father's purpose, and he stayed in his father's presence.[7] Therefore, he was given all the power he needed to complete the work he was given to do.[8] When Jesus was tempted in the wilderness, he overcame Satan and returned to Galilee in the power of the Spirit.[9] At one point in Jesus' ministry, so much power was coming out from him that everyone was trying to touch him for healing.[10]

Here's an amazing thing about Jesus: he used all of his power and all of his resources to serve the needs of those around him, accomplishing his father's goal of saving the world through him. He did not lord it over those he knew. What might be even more amazing is the same power that resides in Jesus has been poured out for us, his disciples, as well. After Jesus' resurrection, he told the disciples, "stay in the city until you have been clothed with power from on high."[11] Have you ever wondered what this really means? My conclusion is that we have the same indwelling power of the Holy Spirit that Jesus did while on earth. No longer does God only dwell in clouds and pillars of fire. As he chose to live in Jesus, he chooses to live in us!

Of course, Jesus was given the Spirit without many limits that we face, for whatever reason. Nevertheless, we have the power of God's name, the power and indwelling of the Holy Spirit, the power of the gospel, the power of hope, joy, and peace, and the power of the resurrection.[12] Wouldn't we, as Christians, be among the most pitied people in the world if we had no power? Wouldn't Jesus be a mockery for the human race if he had no power to do what he preached he would do? The apostle Paul argues that if God's power, shown particularly in the resurrection of Christ, is false, our faith is futile and we are to be pitied.[13]

Consider this: Jesus was born into a household of Jewish working class parents under Roman rule. There was nothing about his appearance that should have made anyone like him.[14] He worked for thirty years as an obedient son and carpenter. At thirty, he called twelve men in the marketplace to his cause and suggested that, with his leadership, they were going to help save the world and call people back to God. And soon the Pharisees were saying, "If we let him go on like this, everyone will put their trust in him."[15] Two thousand years later, this small grassroots movement has brought hope to billions of people.

One of the reasons Jesus continues to be a lightning rod in today's culture is because he wields tremendous power. This power is not oppressive or flashy: Jesus' continual seeking of God's will was an act of power; his forgiveness of the adulteress woman was an act of power; his submission to the cross was the most courageous and powerful act of leadership in human history.

Blaine Lee, in his book *The Power Principle: Influence with Honor,* suggests that power permeates every aspect of our lives. Everyone wields it and everyone is subject to it, because all of us are interconnected. "We live together, work together, shop together, worship together, and play together. In all these settings, we are with other people whose feelings, views, desires, goals, and values may be different from ours. When we come together, it is natural that we influence and are influenced by each other. Power is our ability to influence one another."[16]

Though people have a difficult time defining power and have mixed emotions about it, they can almost always tell you who has it. Just ask ten people in an office setting who has power. The list is easy to create. If you ask people down at city hall who has power, no one will hesitate to tell you. Power is all around us. We know it. We see it. We feel it.

One way to understand power is to consider types of power and relate to them in your own life. Most can clearly identify with the three types of power listed here:

1. **Coercive power.** This type of power controls others' behavior, but only as long as we force them. Once the ability to force people to comply is gone, so is the power.

2. **Utility power.** This power is based on what you can do for another and what they can do for you. Each individual wields power by providing utility or value in someone's life. Utility power is centered on independence as each person tends to look out for his or her own interests.

3. **Principle-centered power.** This power results from honor extended to you from others and by you to others. Principle-centered power lasts over extended periods of time. When people honor each other, there is a trust that leads to synergy, interdependence, and deep respect.[17]

Lee rightly focuses on principle-centered leadership and bases of power, but I believe his beginning point for great power is flawed. He says the beginning point of power is all about you.

After all, his introductory chapter is entitled "The Answer Is In You." I disagree. It's not about you! It's about God.

Look at Jesus and power. What made him distinctive? He did not say, "the answer is in you." Instead, Jesus clearly understood that his power came from above. He "knew the Father had put all things under his power, and that he had come from God and was returning to God."[18] He knew he had a powerful purpose and was returning to the ultimate giver of power, his heavenly father.

Since a servant is no greater than his master, we believe and do as we see our master, Jesus Christ, doing. We too should know that any lasting power comes from above. We came from God and we return to God, the ultimate source of all power.

If you are going to build a brand that matters, you must think rightly about power. God's power is always given to his people to accomplish his purposes. God showed his power to Israel and to Egypt in plagues and miracles to save Israel from slavery in Egypt. Later in Israel's history, King Saul was changed into a different person by the power of the Lord—"The spirit of the Lord will come upon you in power, and you will prophesy with them; and you will be changed into a different person."[19] King David gained power to govern when the "Spirit of the Lord came upon David in power."[20]

In fact, David praises the Lord for his power. He proclaims it in the presence of the whole assembly, ". . . Yours, O Lord, is the greatness and the power and the glory and the majesty and the splendor, for everything in heaven and earth is yours . . . In your hand are strength and power to exalt and give strength to all."[21] In his deep suffering, Job proclaims the moral strength of the Lord when he says, "I will teach you about the power of God; the ways of the almighty I will not conceal."[22]

Do you really believe God would give us the extraordinary task of using our positions to build a brand of leadership that matters, asking us to lead the world to Jesus, without the sufficient power to do so? God has given us everything we need to lead, if we will stay in his purpose and in his presence, using his resources to honor him by leading and serving those within our influence.

God's call is excellence. His brand matters. He commands us to add value. He bids us to be powerful leaders.

We all have the problem of feeling ordinary. Most of us hesitate to accept authentic authority and responsibility, because the calls to be made on the court of life are difficult at best, painful and seemingly impossible at worst. Play on the court is swift, strong, complex, and dominated by powerful forces. *We must find the power of God!*

That's right! Find it! It is the most difficult thing in life I have yet to attempt. But, through years of experience, failure, study, and reflection, I am convinced this is how you do it:

1. Begin with humility.
2. Seek God's presence.
3. Encounter God's glory.
4. Receive power from the Holy Spirit.

This process is easier said than done, and it is at the heart of the matter to which we turn in the next chapter.

Key Points

1. Power and influence are central to leadership.
2. God's brand of leadership has power!
3. Many people are afraid of power.
4. Power in and of itself is neither good nor bad.
5. There are a variety of power types.
6. Christians are powerful people.
7. Jesus is God's brand representative and the world's most powerful leader, leading today in the hearts of more than a third of the world's population.

Challenge

Moses spoke often about the power of God. He proclaimed that the children of Israel were delivered from Egyptian bondage with great power and an outstretched hand.[23] The prophet Samuel spoke to Saul regarding power. He said that Saul would become a different person when the Lord came upon him in power and strength. God's power was given to Saul when he became king and then removed from Saul and given to David after the Lord took the throne from Saul for disobedience.[24]

Before Jehoshaphat defeated Moab and Ammon, he proclaimed, "O Lord, God of our fathers, are you not the God who is in heaven? You rule over all the kingdoms of the nations. Power and might are in your hand, and no one can withstand you."[25] Job declares of God, "His wisdom is profound, his power is vast. Who has resisted him and come out unscathed? He moves mountains without their knowing it and overturns them in his anger."[26] David said, "Your arm is endued with power; your hand is strong, your right hand exalted."[27]

After the temptations in the wilderness, "Jesus returned to Galilee in the power of the Spirit."[28] He gave his disciples authority to overcome all the power of the enemy.[29] He told them they would receive power to be his witnesses in Jerusalem, and in all Judea and Samaria, and to the ends of the earth when the gift of the Holy Spirit came to them.[30]

The Bible is replete with discussions and stories and teachings about power. But, do you personally and truly believe you have access to that same power? Do you really have power to overcome the evil one and his mighty schemes? Do you really think God's power can make you a distinctive leader, enabling you to build a brand of leadership that creates value and has power to change the lives of those you love and lead? Is his power something you can know? If you are unsure, you better take a look at your Bible anew and discover his promised power!

Exploring Big Ideas

1. Define power. Explain why people don't understand it or talk about it.

2. Describe the differences you see between powerful leaders and powerless leaders.

3. Where is power obtained? What factors contribute to creating power in leadership?

4. Describe a time when you felt powerful. Explain why.

5. Describe a time when you felt particularly powerless. Explain why.

6. Why is power most often thought of as negative?

7. Describe Jesus' power. What was his power source?

Chapter Nine

POWER UP

God opposes the proud but gives grace to the humble.

—1 PETER 5:5

We all have *the* problem. God's call is excellence. His brand matters. He commands us to add value. We are ordinary. He bids us to be powerful leaders. We are powerless. We have been asked to officiate on the "court of life"! We would rather not. Most of us are ordinary and don't want authentic authority and responsibility. The calls to be made on the court of life are difficult, at best. Play on the court is swift, strong, complex, and dominated by powerful forces. Besides, each of us is challenged with static cling.

The answer to the power problem is simple yet profound. At first, it may seem to lack intellectual rigor and depth. Perhaps it will seem vague. However, it is real, deep, and complex. It will make you distinctive and your leadership brand exemplary. It will give you power. It will change your life. It will literally give you the brand of God. His mark will be pressed on your soul and you will begin to change the lives of those around you. This answer is the deepest truth I have ascertained to this point in my life. Here it is. Ready? *Find the power of God!*

That's right! Find it! It is the most difficult thing in life I have yet to attempt. But, through years of study, I am convinced that this is how you do it. First, begin with humility. Second, seek God's presence. Third, encounter his glory. Finally, receive power through the indwelling of the Holy Spirit. Did you get it? Whoa! Let's take a look.

Humility

One day, years ago, an elderly couple entered the lobby of a small Philadelphia hotel. "All the big places are filled," the man said. "Can you give us a room?" The clerk said, "Look, there are three conventions in town. There have been no rooms available for weeks. Every guest room in the town is taken. But I can't send a nice couple like you out on a night like this. Would you be willing to sleep in my room?" The next morning as he paid his bill, the elderly man said to the clerk, "You're the kind of manager who should be the boss of the best hotel in the United States, and one day I'm going to build it for you." The clerk laughed and forgot about the incident.

Two years later, the clerk received a letter with a round-trip ticket to New York City and a request to be the guest of the couple whom he had befriended. Once in New York, the old man led the clerk to the corner of 5th street and 34th street and showed him an incredible new building. He declared, "This is the hotel that I built for you to manage." The young man, George C. Boldt, accepted the offer of William Waldorf Astor to become the manager of the original Waldorf Astoria Hotel, widely considered the finest hotel in the world at the time.

———◦———

Henry Cloud said that humility is "not having a need to be more than you are."[1] For me, humility understands the ability to be more than you are is not within you. It is within him. The power is within and from God. In reality, true power begins with humility and results from:

1. A proper view of self
2. A proper view of others
3. A spirit of obedience

Proper View of Self

In first grade, my mom made my lunch most days. One day, though, I had the privilege of walking through the lunch line with the other kids. With tray in hand, I ordered a hot dog and canned corn, and I remember how the excitement built as I neared the end of the line, knowing dessert was coming!

The "dessert lady" looked at me and asked what I would like. I pointed my finger to the dessert area and said "fan-e-law" please. She looked quite puzzled. I didn't know why.

"Excuse me," she said. "What did you say?"

I repeated myself, "I would like some 'fan-e-law' please." Clearly, she wasn't getting it! She looked frustrated with me. So I moved closer and pointed to the vanilla ice cream.

"Oh, VAN-I-LLA!" she said.

"Yes." I said, thinking to myself, *Oh, is that how you say it?* I didn't know. I just pronounced it the way my mom did.

I grew up with parents who could not tell me how to pronounce such words. Mom's eardrums and nerve endings were destroyed by scarlet fever. She knows no sound at all. My dad apparently lost his hearing by falling down a staircase at his home in Detroit. They both lived and learned in a completely silent world.

I experienced my parents as beautifully silent people who pronounced words such as vanilla, "fan-e-law." The rest of us learn to pronounce words by simultaneously listening to and looking at words. Not Mom and Dad. They learned to speak by feeling voice vibrations, watching throat and lip movements, and by seeing related words on the page. Evidently, vanilla wasn't one my mother's best accomplishments. If you have *never* heard a sound, you might imagine it would be quite difficult to articulate the difference between an "f" which has sort of a soft blowing sound and a "v," which has a more guttural sound.

For our family, Dad and Mom have their famous mispronounced words. Dad always pronounced scenery with a hard "k," commenting on the beautiful "ski-nery" as we traveled together. Michelle, our youngest daughter, was often confused because Dad used to call her "Mitchell." He never mastered the difference between soft and hard sounds. Mom often speaks about a smell in the "hair." She means "air." Regardless, shampoo was always on my shopping list growing up. I didn't want Mom talking publicly with her friends about the smell in my hair!

Once, while preparing for our family's participation in a traditional Fourth of July parade in Harbor Springs, Michigan, I blew my daughter's trumpet as loudly as I could about two inches from my mother's left ear. To the amazement of family and friends watching, Mom didn't hear a thing! She only sensed the oily stench that was exhausted as I blew. Those watching were a bit miffed that I would do such a thing, as they cringed at the thought of the sound in their own ears. But Mom laughed, as she always does. She really is deaf.

At eighty four years old, before he died, Dad still had difficulty setting the appropriate volume of his voice for a given situation. Some of my most embarrassing moments during my growing up years were when Dad would enter a church setting, a funeral home, a parent/teacher meeting, my office, or some museum with us and belt out his first sentence at a volume that would attract most police officers on duty.

Because of their handicap of being deaf in a hearing world, it was difficult for my parents to think more highly of themselves than they ought. They were humble people. Thus, they were powerful people. As a result of being raised by handicapped parents, I am acutely aware of my own handicaps and limitations, which is good for me. The truth is that while some handicaps are more noticeable than others, everyone has them. Because my parents understood their limitations, and because they saw different dreams for themselves, my parents were distinctively different and powerful!

Mom entered kindergarten when she was seven years old. She could quickly tell that she was older, taller, and bigger than all the other five-year-old children. When she didn't understand the teacher, she was punished and placed alone in a dark closet in the schoolhouse. Thus, she reasoned, she must be retarded in some way. But Mom had a different idea. She worked hard to overcome her limitations. Eventually, she went on to become valedictorian of the 8th grade class—her highest level of formal education. And in the 1930s, for more than three years, she traveled to Chicago and Minnesota to prove to state legislators that deaf people could, indeed, speak.

Dad was extremely limited. His communication skills were quite an obstacle for him. Yet because of his parents' dream (their big idea) and his willingness to pursue that dream, he became the first deaf person ever to be employed at Ford Motor Company. For a while, he worked in the machine shop as a blue collar worker on the factory floor. However, he had a vision of becoming a white-collar employee with Ford, wanting to be home at nights with my mom and my brothers and me. He was the first deaf person to enroll in a Ford Motor Company trade school. His idea was to become a draftsman, working in the engineering building in the company's world headquarters in Dearborn, Michigan.

After five years of trade school at night, after work, without an interpreter, Dad became the first white collar deaf person to be employed at Ford. It wasn't easy. Dad failed his fourth year and didn't graduate on time. But through the leadership of his mother and father, he went back to school to take the fifth year over again. He passed with an eighty-three average!

He was placed as the first white collar deaf person to be employed by Ford on the drafting floor in Dearborn, but was given a two-week probationary period. On his first day at work, his new boss told him if he didn't perform, he would have to go back to the factory. No pressure, buddy! Dad went on to work for more than forty-two years with Ford as a draftsman in engineering at their world headquarters; by the time he retired, he was supervising twenty-six people.

Additionally, Dad and Mom and my two older brothers made a 1958 front cover of Ford Motor Company's worldwide magazine, *The Ford Times*, for his craftsmanship in creating what may have been the first motor home for camping in the U.S. He purchased an old Detroit city bus for three hundred dollars, restored the engine, and created a design that converted it to become a camping home on wheels for Mom and my brothers.

Mom and Dad lived lives that mattered. They raised three sons who continue to walk with Jesus, they found favor with seven grandchildren and nine great-grandchildren, they nourished a loving marriage for fifty-nine years, and they remained faithful to the Lord all their lives. Their influence has enriched the lives of scores of deaf people across the country and just about everyone with whom they come in contact.

Highly educated? No. Famous? No. Wealthy? No. Advantaged? No. Humble? Yes! Branded? Yes! Powerful? Yes!

Even Jesus did not think of himself with arrogance. I believe one of the reasons Jesus was born in a stable in Bethlehem is because it would be difficult to consider oneself equal with God while lying in a feeding trough! Humility infused Jesus' leadership; he was always pointing people up the chain of command to God.

Even though Jesus was God, he did not consider himself equal with God. He said it on many occasions; "the Father is greater than I,"[2] "no servant is greater than his master,"[3] "the world must learn that I love the Father and that

I do exactly what my Father has commanded me,"[4] and "honor your father and mother."[5] Jesus knew that there was power in this view, which is why he taught his disciples "the least among you is the greatest."[6]

Look at the enduring song about Christ in Philippians 2:5–8:

> Your attitude should be the same as that of Christ Jesus:
> Who, being in very nature God,
> did not consider equality with God something to be grasped,
> but made himself nothing,
> taking the very nature of a servant,
> being made in human likeness.
> And being found in appearance as a man,
> he humbled himself and became obedient
> to death—even death on a cross!

A humble posture before God opens the door for his working in your life. We must embrace this attitude with all our hearts, minds, and strengths in order to be powerful leaders!

Most of us begin building our brand of leadership focused on our positions, thinking more highly of ourselves than we ought. We focus on accomplishments and ambitions. Thus, our needs become paramount. Our performance becomes our focus. Instead, our leadership brand-building adventure should begin with sober judgment. Sober judgment breaks down arrogance, which opens a window of truth and gives you wisdom to discern reality. As servants of God, we are nowhere close to God. We should not consider equality with God something to be grasped. We must remember, with humility and conviction, that we are not God. As James wrote, "humble yourself before the Lord, and He will lift you up."[7]

Collins's research suggests great leaders "channel their ego needs away from themselves and into the larger goal of building a great company [organization]. It's not that [they] have no ego or self-interest. Indeed, they are incredibly ambitious—but their ambition is first and foremost for the institution, not themselves."[8]

He goes on to say people are divided into two categories: "Those who do not have the seed of [greatness] and those who do. The first category consists of people who could never in a million years bring themselves to subjugate their egoistic needs to the greater ambition of building something larger and more lasting than themselves. For these people, work will always be first and foremost about what they get—fame, fortune, adulation, power, whatever—not what they build, create, and contribute."[9]

What about you? Are you humble? Do you know for certain that you are not God? Do you respect and revere God? Do you fear, respect, and honor his holiness? Do you beg for his presence? Do you seek his favor and his forgiveness? God is a fair judge and knows our hearts. Examples in Scripture show that people who do these things found favor in the eyes of the Lord, and you can find favor in God's eyes, as well.

Building a brand of leadership that matters requires a daily acknowledgment of limitations before God. Those with humility ponder each day the reality that the power to achieve success is not within them, but in Jesus Christ.

A Proper View of Others

I deeply admire one particular trustee of Abilene Christian University, Randy Nicholson. He was raised an orphan in Texas and sent to Abilene Christian University by some kindhearted women from his church. These women believed that he needed a Christian education, so they funded it themselves. Today, some fifty years later, he is a child of God and a successful husband, father, and businessman. He and his wife recently pledged a multimillion-dollar gift to the College of Business Administration at Abilene Christian University. When I asked him why he gave this gift to ACU, he replied, "I know where I came from. I started with nothing. I had no family, no friends, no hope, and no future. Everything I have today, my faith, my wife, my daughter, my friends, my business associates, and my church family came from the good Lord and ACU. I began with nothing. I know it all came from the Lord."

Because Jesus understood himself before God, he was able to have a proper attitude toward others. He consistently proclaimed, "I am the good shepherd. The good shepherd lays down his life for the sheep . . . The reason my Father loves me is that I lay down my life—only to take it up again."[10] He lived and embodied what John Maxwell calls the Law of Sacrifice, leaders sacrificing on behalf of others. If you follow Jesus, you must give up to go up! Amazingly, Jesus claimed all those that God claimed for him.[11] He claimed the rich, the poor, the wealthy, the sick, the healthy, the powerful, and the powerless. This is not easy for me to do. I have a hard time getting a proper view of myself, and so, too often, I get my view of others all messed up.

One Christmas, my family and I attended church with my parents. At the time, the church was new and meeting in a school building near my parents' home. As we entered, we were greeted by several nice people welcoming us to worship services.

Once inside the school, I noticed something. These people seemed a bit different. I didn't know what it was at first. However, after some time with them, I determined that they were a bit backward. I mean, the interpreter seemed nice, but she needed some help with "style." The children seemed to be dressed about twenty years behind the times. When the song leader got up to lead singing, he tucked his songbook under his stub arm and led with his other hand. The singing was . . . not that good.

As the preacher began his lesson, I noticed that his suit coat was old and mis-buttoned. His top button on the right side was attached to the second hole on the left side of his coat. He had a brush cut hairstyle like my brothers had in the 1950s. As he preached, he continually forgot where he was in his notes. Distressed, I thought to myself, "My parents deserve better than this!"

Yet at that moment, thinking about Jesus and the cross, my spirit was convicted of sin like few times before. Here I was, standing in judgment because these people did not meet my "standards" of living and worshiping. Jesus sweetly said to me, "blessed are the poor in spirit, for theirs is the Kingdom of heaven."[12] More of his words poured out: "Judge not, lest ye be judged"; "If any of you offers a cup of cold water in my name, he is offering it to me"; "Whoever acknowledges me before men, I will acknowledge before my father in heaven." On and on the word of the Lord convicted me of my sin. Tears filled the wrinkles in my skin and ran down my cheeks like cleansing rain.

The people in this church were acknowledging Jesus as Lord, and I knew he claimed them as his own. My condescending view revealed my sin: a flawed view of others. "Oh God, I can never lead like Jesus did!" I thought. And, on my own, I can't. But Jesus teaches us how to serve out of love because he represents the God of the universe serving people to the greatest extent of his love. This is real power from on high.

A Spirit of Obedience

Carlos Sepulveda, as CEO of Interstate Batteries, told my business students that obedience helped him achieve his current position as CEO. His first job was working as a grocery store clerk. On his first day, the boss told him to sweep under the candy racks every night before he went home. Carlos obeyed.

Night after night, Carlos swept under the candy racks before he went home. He wondered how everyone else completed their tasks and went home much sooner than he. After about two weeks, some employees asked him why he was sweeping under the candy racks every night.

"The boss told me," he said. They explained to Carlos that the boss told everyone to sweep under the candy racks, but nobody really did it.

Two months later, Carlos was the boss of his fellow employees—and they were sweeping under the candy racks every night!

Carlos Sepulveda's obedience helped him rise to influential positions of leadership.

Have you ever wondered where our teaching on "obedience" has gone? Can you remember the last time you heard a prominent leader talk about obedience? What about the last time you heard a good sermon on the virtue and power of obedience? We tend to get a bit of it after a business scandal breaks, or a television evangelist is exposed for fraud, or a government official gets caught in an affair. But most of the time, we don't contemplate or espouse the importance of obedience to the health of our families, marriages, churches, businesses, and society!

Jesus said, "be faithful in the little things, and I will make you faithful over many."[13] Paul reiterated the idea, writing, "Now it is required that those who have been given a trust must prove faithful."[14] As I examine the lives of Noah, Abraham, Joseph, Moses, David, and Jesus, I find a clear connection between obedience and power. In fact, in every instance, a lifetime of obedience comes before God grants his favor of presence and power. Jesus was obedient to his parents, and he "grew in wisdom, stature, and favor with God and man."[15] He was obedient to God's will during his testing in the wilderness with Satan.[16] He repeatedly said, "I do nothing on my own ... I always do what pleases him."[17] To his listeners, he says, "if anyone loves me, he will obey my teaching. My father will love him and we will come and make our home with him. He who does not love me will not obey my teaching."[18]

Can you imagine what your home would be like if Jesus and God came and lived with you? My, how things would change! I bet the conversations would be a little sweeter. The television would probably be in the "off" position more. And your checkbook would probably be altered significantly.

Samuel told Saul, "To obey is better than sacrifice, and to heed is better than the fat of rams."[19] Obedience in light of God's sovereignty is what pleases the Lord! Here is one of Jesus' last commandments for us to obey: "Therefore go and make disciples of all nations, baptizing them in the name of the Father and of the Son and of the Holy Spirit, and teaching them to obey everything I have commanded you. And surely I am with you always, to the very end of the age."

How are you doing? Power begins with humility!

Key Points

1. Power begins with humility.
2. Power results from a proper view of one's self before God, a proper view of others, and a spirit of obedience.
3. Jesus models all these attitudes.
4. The power of Jesus had less to do with his position among men and more to do with his posture before God.
5. Limitations never prevent anyone from achieving greatness. Failing to acknowledge your limitations does!
6. Building a brand of leadership that matters requires a daily acknowledgment of limitations before God.
7. Arrogance precludes truth and discernment.

Challenge

Jesus' power was literally out of this world! He knew his position relative to God and others, and as a result, he was able to fulfill his eternal destiny. His attitude provided clarity of purpose few of us find today. It gave him an unprecedented ability to become exactly what God wanted him to become—a powerful lover of people. He knew that he came from God and was returning to God. He came to seek and save that which was lost. He came not to be served, but to serve and give his life as a ransom for many.

Interestingly, Jesus had no fear proclaiming who he was—savior of the world! His humility can be seen in the way he treated his father in heaven with deference and respect, always speaking highly of his father and always acknowledging his sovereignty and power. Because he understood his position before his father in heaven, he was able to serve others in ways that continue to defy human ability and will.

For us, the beginning of power arrives when we develop the same attitude as that of Christ Jesus: a reverent view of God and others and incessant obedience to God's will.

Exploring Big Ideas

1. Describe why the attitude of Jesus is so difficult to develop.

2. What is it about our human spirit or the spirit of the world that inhibits our humility?

3. Note some examples of humility in leaders you know. Do you desire to follow these people?

4. How did Jesus develop and maintain his humility?

5. How did Jesus' attitude contribute toward success in fulfilling God's will for him on earth?

6. List all the things about Jesus' attitude that resulted in greatness.

7. How do limitations become factors that can contribute to greatness?

Chapter Ten

POWER ON

What else will distinguish me and your people
from all the other people on the face of the earth?
Now, show me your glory!

—EXODUS 33:16, 18

Rebuilt Parts and Lives

Michael Cardone, Jr., is president and CEO of Cardone Industries, Inc., in Philadelphia, Pennsylvania. Cardone Industries, Inc., is a leading remanufacturer of automotive parts for the aftermarket. They focus on six basic product lines: brakes (master cylinders, calipers), drivetrain parts (constant-velocity drive axles), electronics (climate and spark controls, fuel-display modules), motors (window-lift and wiper), pumps (water and vacuum), and steering (rack and pinion units, power-steering filters). The company remanufactures its products in Pennsylvania and has warehouse facilities in California, as well as Belgium and Canada. The Cardone family controls the business.

Mr. Cardone employs approximately four thousand workers in twenty different factories comprised of twenty-five different nationalities and seventeen different languages. Many of the people employed are considered unemployable by other companies in town. Mr. Cardone takes them in, offers them work-skills training and professional development, and attempts to give them the benefits of being part of a large loving family. He offers Christian teaching to those who seek it and has daily Bible devotionals to start the workday for any employee who wants to participate.

His factories and offices have served as the physical locations for numerous weddings, funerals, and church services. In fact, one church used a factory

127

facility as their primary place of worship because the inner city churches in Philadelphia didn't want all the ethnic minorities that were being converted to Christianity in their assemblies on Sunday. "They didn't have room," the church leaders told Mr. Cardone.

Why does Michael Cardone act this way? For one thing, he is another example of someone who faces physical challenges—and uses his circumstances to help him stay focused on lasting goals. Cardone was born with a rare disease that paralyzed half of his face. Today, he speaks with a lazy cheek that puffs air as he talks. His nose is disfigured. He says he graduated fifty-ninth out of a class of sixty students in his high school. The other guy, he says with a smile, dropped out. Mr. Cardone knows he is not God, and constantly gives thanks for God's sovereignty, goodness, and mercy. Cardone's power has accomplished wonderful things.

When you are humble, you are pliable. When you are pliable, God can do powerful things with you and through you. I am not there yet. Most of us are not.

One might conclude that by the time the Israelites made it across the Red Sea, Moses was a fairly confident, seasoned, and powerful leader. To the contrary, subsequent to these events, Moses says to the Lord, "You have been telling me, 'Lead these people,' but you have not let me know whom you will send with me."[1] Come on, Moses! What do you mean you don't know who will go with you? Who has been with you all along? It's been God, hasn't it? You know that!

Yes—God had been there all along. But something had been missing in the relationship. If you look at the text carefully, Moses articulates that God knew him by name and had found favor with him, but *Moses* still didn't know *God*! In Moses's continuous quest for greatness and power he was frustrated and fearful because he only knew the acts or works of God. So he asks God to teach him his ways so that he might know him and continue to find favor with him.[2] The Lord replies, "My Presence will go with you, and I will give you rest."[3]

Moses didn't get it. (As I so often don't.) So, he again pleads, "If your presence does not go with us, do not send us up from here. How will anyone know that you are pleased with me and with your people unless you go with us? What else will distinguish me and your people from all the other people on the face of the earth?"[4] Moses is begging for a brand.

Again, God attempts to reassure Moses and says, "I will do the very thing you have asked, I am pleased with you and I know you by name."[5] Still unconvinced that anything significant has been accomplished in this dialogue, Moses pushes further.

"Now show me your glory," Moses says.[6] Don't you wonder why Moses asks to see God's glory? I believe Moses wanted to be at the very center of God's presence and power. He wanted to *see* God's power. He wanted to *know* God. And he got what he wanted:

> And the Lord said, "I will cause all my goodness to pass in front of you, and I will proclaim my name, the Lord, in your presence. I will have mercy on whom I will have mercy, and I will have compassion on whom I will have compassion. But," he said, "you cannot see my face, for no one may see me and live."
>
> Then the Lord came down in the cloud and stood there with him and proclaimed his name, the Lord. And he passed in front of Moses, proclaiming, "The Lord, the Lord, the compassionate and gracious God, slow to anger, abounding in love and faithfulness, maintaining love to thousands, and forgiving wickedness, rebellion and sin. Yet he does not leave the guilty unpunished; he punishes the children and their children for the sin of the fathers to the third and fourth generation."[7]

Moses was forever changed by that experience, branded by the transforming power of the presence of God. Before this time, Moses doubted God time and again. Even though Moses had seen a host of God's manifestations of power, he constantly doubted his leadership and his ability to carry the grand mission to completion. The whining of the people and the sinful nature of their rebellious hearts discouraged Moses. He often wondered why he was in this game at all.

Once God brands Moses with the power of his presence, Moses never again complains or argues to be released from his work as a leader of the people. Moses's vision is solid. His power source is secure. He is transformed and finally *knows* God! The people take note when they see Moses coming down from his encounter with God: "When Moses came down from Mount Sinai with the two tablets of the Testimony in his hands, he was not aware that his face was radiant because he had spoken with the Lord."[8]

Every time Moses entered God's presence after that, he was changed. His face glowed so that the people asked him to wear a veil: "But, whenever he [Moses] entered the Lord's presence to speak with him, he removed the veil until he came out. And when he came out and told the Israelites what he had been commanded, they saw that his face was radiant."[9] He was like one of those little glow toys you get in a Happy Meal at McDonald's. As long as the toy spends time in the presence of light, it glows when the lights go out. But over time, as it is away from the radiance, it fades.

Moses was now completing the process of moving from good to great, abandoning the ordinary and seeking a distinctive brand of leadership that mattered. He was distinguishing himself and God's people from all other people on the face of the earth. The answer to the dilemma of God's call to greatness and the reality of Moses's own sin and weakness was found in the power of God's glory. Once Moses was able to *know* God, he was finally ready to fulfill his divine appointment without hesitation.

The Power Up Process

If we outline the process by which Moses abandoned the ordinary, powering up for a great finale, it would look like that shown in Table 10.1.

TABLE 10.1 Moses: Finding Power	
Situation	What Moses Learns
1. Moses grows up in a privileged household.	Power of Position
2. Moses renounces Pharoah and lives with the people of God.	Power of Humility
3. Moses murders someone, runs away and hides.	Power of Sin
4. Moses encounters God in the burning bush.	Power of God's Call
5. Moses agrees to lead the children of Israel out of bondage.	Power of Obedience
6. Moses pleads with God to abandon his leadership role.	Power of Fear
7. Moses goes to Pharoah, fearfully leading through plagues, deliverance, and the initial wanderings in the desert.	Power of Obedience
8. Moses continues to plead with God, "I do not know who will go with me and I do not know how to be distinctive."	Power of His Presence
9. Moses asks God to teach him so he might *know* him.	Power of His Presence
10. God favors Moses and agrees to show his glory.	Power of His Presence
11. Moses is transformed, never again displaying fear.	Power of His Presence
12. God completes his mission with Moses, taking him home.	Power of His Presence

An analysis of Moses's life reveals five distinct steps for powering up with God (shown in Table 10.2). First, he humbly obeyed God with everything he had—his heart, mind, soul, and strength. Though often afraid and unwilling in spirit, Moses did what God asked him to do. Second, through a lifetime of struggle, humility, and obedience, Moses earnestly sought and ran after the presence of God. Third, because of his obedience and aggressive pursuit of a relationship with God, Moses found favor with God. Fourth, because Moses found favor with God, he is invited to encounter God's glory. Finally, Moses powers up through receiving God's power!

TABLE 10.2 Moses's Power Up Process	
Step 1	Humble Obedience
Step 2	Seek His Presence
Step 3	Find His Favor
Step 4	Encounter His Glory
Step 5	Receive His Power

Elements of this process can also be found in the words of Jesus as he neared the completion of his time on earth. He prayed,

> Father, the time has come. Glorify your Son, that your Son may glorify you. For you granted him authority over all people that he might give eternal life to all those you have given him. Now this is eternal life; that they may know you, the only true God, and Jesus Christ, whom you have sent. I have brought you glory on earth by completing the work you gave me to do. And now, Father, glorify me in your presence with the glory I had with you before the world began.[10]

In the same way God dealt with Moses, Jesus brought Peter, James, and John close to witness his glory. He gathered them on a mountain and saw that "his face shone like the sun, and his clothes became as white as the light."[11] It's probably no coincidence that Jesus' "power up" session (transfiguration) with his disciples included an appearance by Moses. Both men were radiant because of the presence and power of God!

Remarkably, we too have access to God's presence. In fact, God has gifted us even more than Moses, for God no longer confines his presence to a cloud or a pillar of fire, as he did in Moses's day. He has gifted us with the permanent indwelling and presence of his Holy Spirit: "We are not like Moses, who would put a veil over his face to keep the Israelites from gazing at it while the radiance was fading away . . . ," rather, ". . . we, who with unveiled faces all reflect the Lord's glory, are being transformed into his likeness with ever increasing glory, which comes from the Lord, who is the Spirit."[12]

Once in God's presence, we will be transformed by his glory. Notice I state emphatically that we *will* be transformed into his likeness. Look at Paul's words again: "Whenever, anyone turns to the Lord, the veil is taken away. Now the Lord is spirit, and where the Spirit of the Lord is, there is freedom. And we, who with unveiled faces all reflect the Lord's glory, are being transformed into his likeness with ever-increasing glory, which comes from the Lord, who is the Spirit."[13]

If you are in the presence of God, you will be changed. When the Lord called Moses to lead the children of Israel out of bondage, he was told that "I Am" would be with him. Moses kept saying, Lord, I can't lead these people. I am not properly equipped for leadership. I can't help it. It's just the way "I am." In essence, God responds by saying, it may be the way you are now, but if my presence goes with you, you will change. Tell Pharaoh and the people you are leading, I Am who I Am, and in my presence, all others must change.

One of the most common excuses among us today is "that's just the way I am." We use it to provide justification for improper attitudes and actions. Someone might say, "I was born with a hot temper, and I have just never been able to control it. That's just how I am, and there's nothing I can do about it!" The real fallacy in all this is that God is the only "I AM"; the rest of us were created to *become*.

The apostle Peter had a quick temper. He drew his sword in a heartbeat and attacked Malchus in a fight against people who would take his master. A quick temper was obviously a part of his character, but he was not locked in. Over time, he became a man of steady attitudes and actions, the rock Jesus called him to be.

John liked revenge. When a certain village refused to hear the preaching of Jesus, John's response was to call down fire from heaven and destroy them. He wanted to get even with these people because they had hurt him. That is the way

John was. However, it is not the way John remained. He became the man who was known as the apostle of love, writing more than anyone else in the Bible about love and patience for others.

As we seek God's presence, contemplating his divine splendor and goodness, we will come to know him and be changed through the power of the Holy Spirit. How can we not be changed if we stand in the presence of this power? It's like standing in the presence of the sun outside. All you need to do is expose your skin to the sun, and it will be changed. This is not a probability; it's fundamental science. The change will occur in you, but the power to change will come from above you. Many miraculous things happen when you are exposed to the power of the sun, and none of it come from your power, other than your role in seeking the exposure. Sunlight adds vitamin D to your body, darkens your skin color, lightens your hair color. In similar fashion, we are transformed when we find ourselves exposed to God—not through our power, but through God's.

Conclusion

The glory of Christ is a mystery.[14] Over and over, the writers of the New Testament reiterate this point. Therefore, we should not expect the power of God's presence and the deep riches of his wisdom—qualities we need to develop distinctive leadership—to be easily found. We must search these out. That's why Paul said, "I keep asking that the God of our Lord Jesus Christ, the glorious father, may give you the Spirit of wisdom and revelation, so that you might know him better."[15]

Moses wanted to *know* God. Therefore, God showed Moses his mysterious glory and granted his presence and power. It was the same in the New Testament: "To those whom God chooses to disclose the riches of his glory, he makes known the mystery, which is Christ in you, the hope of glory."[16]

When you see God in all his glory, you will have the power to abandon the ordinary. Do you see anything yet? Power Up!

Heading into the fourth and final section of the book, I challenge you to take your distinctive foundation of perspective, position, and power, and add a distinctive set of promises to be embraced and daily managed by you. This set of distinctive promises is your personal signature of gifts, talents, and brand attributes God has given you for each of your positions in life. Let's finish it!

Key Points

1. To power up with God, you must humble yourself before him.
2. The distinctive power of God is his glory.
3. God's glory is only revealed when one enters his presence.
4. God grants his presence to those who earnestly seek and find his favor.
5. Obedience precedes his favor.
6. Power results from "Son" exposure.
7. Powerful transformation happens to us. It is not something we do to ourselves.

Challenge

Do you really believe that spending time in God's presence will change you? Do you really understand that the presence of another changes you? Why is it that we want our kids to hang around other good kids? Because we know that the presence of good is an influence for good. Recently, I was attempting to recruit a faculty member to our college. This individual has three nationally recognized business textbooks. He is a world-class teacher and international scholar and lecturer. His name, Dr. J. William Petty, is noted often for his work in entrepreneurship at home and abroad. Beyond that he has the sweet spirit of Jesus Christ. I knew he would be a great asset to our entire work simply because of his presence on our faculty. If our faculty could spend time with him, watch him, learn from him, and see him work, they would be changed for the better. I know it to be true.

Unfortunately, many of us fear the presence of those who excel beyond us in a variety of ways. We find them intimidating. However, being in the presence of those who have excelled allows us to become better ourselves. That's why Jesus came and spent time with the twelve disciples. They needed his presence in their lives. Spending hours and hours with the master teacher changed them for eternity.

Are you honestly and passionately spending time seeking the presence of God? Are you obedient to his teachings? Are you faithful in what he has given you to this point? Are you looking for ways to spend time with the master, allowing his presence to change you?

Exploring Big Ideas

1. Why is the presence of God so important to becoming a powerful leader?

2. Why do so many people think God's presence is granted like fast-food at the drive-through?

3. List some reasons you believe God's presence does not go with people today.

4. List characteristics of those who seem to live in the presence of God, reflecting his glory.

5. Articulate the difference between knowing about God and having a personal relationship with him.

6. How might you compare and contrast the presence of God we know about through the Old Testament with the presence of God we learn about in the New Testament? (Consider, for example, Exodus 13:21–22 and 1 Corinthians 2:9ff.)

7. God's presence is only his to grant. Discuss how it is that God grants his presence to people like you and me (see John 14:21–23, Rom. 9:15–16).

Part Four

PROMISE

Chapter Eleven

INTELLECTUAL BANDWIDTH

Choose my instruction instead of silver,
knowledge rather than choice gold.

—PROVERBS 8:10

P romise—the fourth "P," is your personal brand promise: a distinct set of promises you daily embrace, manage, and deliver as you live and lead. Built on the foundation of your first three "P"s, it creates your signature brand of leadership through the unique talents, gifts, and attributes that God has given you.

Our starting point in this final section is your mind and heart. To get us going, let me share a true story. During our Leadership Summit course in Colorado several years back, two students disobeyed orders to stay on the trail. They ended up stranded on a steep, rough, and cold Colorado rocky mountain for five hours one night in January, wearing only T-shirts and sweat pants. Every emergency and rescue unit in Colorado Springs was dispatched to save them. Every backup unit was also called. According to the captain of the rescue team, who was serving in his thirty-seventh year, this was the most dangerous rescue he had ever attempted.

We finally got word that both boys were off the mountain and being brought back down to safety. I asked the paramedics what they would first do to assess the boys' situation. First, they said, they would hug them and then slug them. After that, they would run a series of tests to check for signs of hypothermia. "If the mind and the heart shut down," they said, "life is over."

It's the same with leadership. The mind and heart must be healthy, or the life of the leader is over!

God was gracious to us on that trip in several ways. First, the boys were able to recover completely. Second, we didn't have to pay for the amazing rescue services that saved their lives; the costs were covered by the state. Third, when news of the rescue hit one of the front pages of the *Colorado Springs Gazette*, the boys were said to be from Texas Christian University. Since we were from Abilene Christian University and didn't want our mishap publicized, we were smiling all the way home. This is one time when the lack of a strong national brand worked to our advantage.

Legendary NFL football coach Vince Lombardi once said, "You've got to be smart to be number one in any business. But more important, you've got to play with your heart—with every fiber of your body." It takes both.

———

Let's consider first the power of knowledge in building a leadership brand that matters. Jesus used knowledge to his advantage, demonstrating that people with knowledge have power regardless of their title and position. He chided the Sadducees when he said, "you are in error because you do not know the scriptures or the power of God."[1] These Sadducees were good people who did not possess a knowledge of God; therefore, they had no real power.

As an example of this truth, I will speak of Jozell Brister who wields incredible power in the College of Business Administration because she is smart and has special knowledge. She and I have worked together for nearly eighteen years, and I can attest: no one knows more about the work of our college than Jozell. Her knowledge is invaluable to ACU, the College of Business Administration, and me.

She was there when the college began. She helped design, fund, and build our current world-class facility. She served as associate dean during the formative years of the college. She has been a fundraiser for the school. She knows all about the requirements and stressors of national accreditations. She knows her stuff! I always want her by my side when I am facing tough issues in the college. As Sir Francis Bacon said, "knowledge is power."

In any leadership situation, followers expect leaders to have knowledge about what they are doing together. Incompetence won't cut it. The leader must be the teacher. Indeed, distinctive powerful leaders are teachers. To be a good teacher, one must possess knowledge that is critical to the leadership task at hand. It is the leader's responsibility to raise the collective intelligence of his or her team (whether in business, family, or church) and keep its members aligned, energized, and working to fulfill the vision.

Who wants to follow an incompetent leader? What kind of follower gets excited to listen to the words of a leader who is out of touch and uninformed about important issues related to the leadership assignment? Which of you would follow the lead and advice of a poorly dressed professional clothing salesperson? Who would take the advice of a personal fitness trainer who was overweight and uninformed about diet and exercise?

One time, my brother Bill joined a hunting expedition in Alaska. His group was assigned to a relatively new guide for this particular hunt. Some of the men on the trip were skeptical because of the guide's youth. However, they gave him the benefit of the doubt, having little knowledge of their own and having paid extremely good money to be led to locations where wild game abound.

On day one, weather became an issue. The guide signaled for the group to head back. After some time, many in the group doubted their collective direction. They questioned the guide, but he assured them his GPS was leading them home. As darkness began to fall, Bill pulled his old magnetic Boy Scout compass out of his pocket. He had been monitoring it all day. The compass indicated they were headed the wrong direction. He suggested another route home. The guide disagreed.

At this point, the group had to decide whom to follow. After some discussion, they chose Bill because of his knowledge and extensive hunting background. Once Bill began leading, the guide joined in and followed as well. They returned to camp safely. The power of knowledge is a key to strong and effective leadership, especially when you are in a crisis situation.

Jesus used knowledge power consistently throughout his leadership journey. It was one of his brand's defining characteristics! It underpinned everything he was about. His approach to leadership was undergirded by a solid understanding of the issues of the day and the will of his father in heaven. Even today, many who won't give him their heart will commend his teaching. He is often called the "master teacher," imparting eternal truths for life and leadership.

Jesus' knowledge is one of his trademarks. His teachings are branded. They are unique. They are bold, simple, insightful, and powerful for transformation. When Jesus encountered the religious leaders at the temple, they were drawn to him because of his spiritual knowledge. In fact, "everyone who heard him was amazed at his understanding and his answers."[2] When he encountered Satan in the wilderness during a time of most difficult temptation, Jesus called upon his knowledge to refute Satan. And when he encountered the masses in the marketplace, they "were amazed at his teaching, because he taught as one who had authority, and not as their teachers of the law."[3]

Relatively early in his leadership ministry, Jesus taught about the serious nature of discipleship under his leadership. He explained he was the bread of heaven who came down to give life to the world. Jesus stated that unless the disciples ate of his flesh and drank of his blood, they would have no life in them.[4] Upon hearing this difficult teaching, many of the disciples turned back and no longer followed him. Jesus turned to the twelve and said, "You do not want to leave too, do you?" Simon Peter answered Jesus. "Lord, to whom shall we go? You have the words of eternal life."[5] The lesson: powerful teachings lead many to follow.

Today's Christian community seems to be losing its knowledge power! The word of God is not known as it once was. We don't honor or study the word, contemplating its meaning like previous generations did. It is not hidden in our hearts. I am convinced that, as a nation, we are engaging in activities that promote the current biblical knowledge deficit. It has already impacted our generation and will significantly lessen the power of our leadership in generations to come.

Think about it. First, in many churches, the bulk of our community time is spent in "praise and worship." This is a great thing! Please don't misunderstand. I love the praise and worship time we have developed in our assemblies.

Second, we have changed our kids' programs so that they engage in much the same thing during their time together. Great!

Next, we have really gotten into service! This is great as well. We send missionaries all over the world and strategically go and visit them. Parents go. Kids go. Churches go. Great!

However, we don't spend as much time teaching and contemplating the word of God! We get a fifteen-minute sermonette on Sunday morning, often watered down to "seeker-friendly" status. Unfortunately, this approach has weakened our teachable point of view. We spend little time in rigorous, in-depth, foundational, powerful study in God's word. We have lost our knowledge power. That is why, as a group, our record on the court of life is so terrible!

My studies indicate we are not teaching our children at home either. Broad research reveals that most children spend four to seven hours a day watching television or playing video games, and they're not watching the History and Discovery channels. We're not teaching our children in church as we once did, either. We seem to devote all our teaching time to coloring bags, sending candy to missionaries, and writing notes to elderly people. Great stuff. But what are they learning intellectually? Where's the power?

Too often, we are caving into the temptations of this world. All of us are. Satan is winning against us! We don't have a leg to stand on. We don't know what the word of God says. New converts to Christianity get a soft version of Jesus—one that is not intellectually stimulating. That's why we are losing the battle. We are ignorant in the true sense of the word because we are moving away from that which has the power to save and protect us—the word of God! The early church grew in the marketplace, and then they brought converts into the community of believers to learn what it meant to be transformed into the body of Christ.

If living for Christ and fighting a spiritual battle against Satan can be likened to the mission of a football team, here, in my opinion, is where we stand. A good football coach knows that winning football games is a multifaceted process, needing an aggressive strategy that works on many fronts.

First, the winning team will assemble great leadership. Next, it will take time to engage in excellent recruiting.

Next, it will focus on conditioning: both physical (diet, exercise, and strength training) and mental (knowing the playbook inside and out).

Then it will practice, practice, practice.

As game time approaches and the season's play is about to begin, the team will engage in an in-depth study of opponents and their strategies before formulating a game plan, given their own strengths and weaknesses and the strengths and weaknesses of their opponents.

Finally, the first game day comes, and the band, cheerleaders, and drill team all gather and engage the whole campus in an emotional pep rally. The energy level is high, everyone participates, fans are jumping up and down and waving hands, people are feeling good and having fun, and the stage is set for battle. The coaches and players are excited and motivated to go out and give it their best for themselves and the fans.

My analysis is this: overall, we are engaging mostly in pep rallies in our churches! If a football team only engaged in exciting pep rallies, they would be crushed on the field of play each and every week. They win because they did intensive work to prepare *before* the pep rally.

We are getting crushed on the field of play because we are powerless, not knowing what we need to know. Jesus always responded to Satan and his contemporaries with the word of God. We need to do so as well. We all need to know his playbook. We need to condition. We need to know the opponent. We need to practice. The pep rally is the fun part. The real power lies elsewhere.

Passing It On

Building a brand of leadership that matters results when leaders possess and use knowledge power, passing it on to others. When knowledge is passed along, power is passed along. Today, many pass along corrupt ideas that do not lead to godly power and judgment for the betterment of mankind, the advancement of the kingdom, and the glory of our heavenly father.

Most organizations with any measure of staying power in the marketplace are teaching organizations, those who value knowledge and purposefully design ways to infuse it and pass it along throughout the organization. The leader, using the power of knowledge, actively pursues strategies that produce knowledgeable leaders at every level of the organization.

As the master teacher, Jesus modeled the way for you to pass along knowledge. His whole leadership journey on earth was framed with the perspective and understanding that his mission, to be successful, would need to be fulfilled through a process of discipleship. He was leaving in three years and needed to train a group of people to carry his will after his departure.

In short, here is how he did it. First, he was purposeful. There is that word again. He was focused on constantly teaching others. Every time he could, he taught the masses and the disciples numerous lessons about life on this earth, eternal life, and leadership in the kingdom.

Second, he recruited wisely and focused his energy. He recruited twelve people, graduated eleven, and focused on three. He strategically taught the masses at opportune times, but he didn't reach everyone. There were many who never heard his voice. It would be up to his followers to get the message to the rest.

The overall lesson for you is to do likewise. You should teach the masses at opportune times. In your business, your family, and your church, you need to constantly spread God's teachable point of view to as many as you can. However, God has given you people in your immediate realm of influence, and you need to focus the bulk of your work on them, being involved in leadership development and knowledge transfer with those over whom you have the most influence. Again, the key is to strategically choose whom to work with given your positions, your priorities, and the vision God has given you.

Unfortunately, I think we do the best job of this in our businesses and the worst job in our families and our churches. How much time do you spend working on leadership development in your family? How much time do you spend teaching your children? How much time do churches spend developing leaders at every level of the church? I bet I know the answer: not much! Jesus gave the bulk of his leadership focus to twelve people. Do you think you have the capacity to do more than he did? I think not.

Therefore, I urge you to focus on those positions of leadership that are most important in your life. Spend time in his presence to gain knowledge, use his big ideas to craft a vision given your positions on the court, then proactively and purposefully devote yourselves to developing about a dozen people around you.

Key Points

1. Knowledge is power. It is a force for change.
2. Jesus uses knowledge power to build his brand of leadership. Many know and respect him as one who taught with knowledge and authority.
3. Pep rallies don't win football games and they don't win real games on the court of life.
4. Knowledge of the opponent and the playbook is foundational to the game plan.
5. Knowledge without judgment is vain and judgment without knowledge is irrational.
6. Knowledge puffs up but love builds up.
7. Jesus recruited and taught twelve, graduated eleven, and focused on three. He strategically taught the masses at opportune times, but he didn't teach everyone. There were many who never heard his voice directly.

Challenge

The power that comes from knowledge is most alluring because it has a tendency to puff up one's ego or self-perception, leading to unhealthy and immoral ways. Paul wrote about it when he told the Corinthians, "We know that we all possess knowledge. Knowledge puffs up, but love builds up. The man who thinks he knows something does not yet know as he ought to know. But the man who loves God is known by God."[6]

I wonder what it is, according to the apostle Paul, that we do not know when we think we know something? Perhaps God is teaching us to remember that we are all limited and our knowledge is incomplete. Sometimes our knowledge provides freedom for us that cannot be experienced by others because of their lack of knowledge. This is what tends to puff us up! We know something that others don't. Therefore, we begin to think we are better and more advanced than they. At other times, we are harmful to others due to our lack of knowledge, binding things on others that are not of sound judgment.

I think this quandary is why Jesus told the following story:

Two men went up to the temple to pray, one a Pharisee and the other a tax collector. The Pharisee stood up and prayed about himself: "God, I thank you that I am not like other men—robbers, evildoers, adulterers—or even like this tax collector. I fast twice a week and give a tenth of all I get." But the tax collector stood at a distance. He would not even look up to heaven, but beat his breast and said, "God, have mercy on me, a sinner." I tell you that this man, rather than the other, went home justified before God.[7] For everyone who exalts himself will be humbled, and he who humbles himself will be exalted.[8]

Knowledge power is only most useful when an individual possesses both knowledge and has a heart for God. A lover of God with knowledge power begins to approach the legacy of King David, described as a leader who had both love and knowledge.[9]

Let's remember that knowledge is power. It is a force for change. It is a leadership tool that must be developed and deployed. In the words of Dr. Tichy, "We are traversing terrain that weak or sleazy self-aggrandizers cannot take us across safely. We need *smart*, gutsy leaders with vision and integrity to get us through the minefields."[10] Incompetence won't cut it. The leader must be the teacher. Indeed, powerful leaders who are building a brand of leadership that matters are teachers. To be a good teacher, one must possess knowledge that is critical to the leadership task at hand. It is the leader's responsibility to raise the collective intelligence of the team and keep its members aligned, energized, and working to fulfill the vision.

Exploring Big Ideas

1. Describe why the mind of Jesus is so difficult for us to develop (Rom. 12).

2. How did Jesus condition his mind? Can you list some exercises in which he regularly engaged to maintain and strengthen the condition of his mind?

3. List things about Jesus' mind that resulted in a brand of leadership that mattered.

4. Note some leaders who use knowledge to influence and persuade others effectively.

5. How did Jesus use knowledge power to lead? Can you cite some examples where he used knowledge power, creating a distinctive leadership moment?

6. In 1 Corinthians 8:1–3, why do you think the apostle Paul stated that knowledge puffs up?

7. How could one lead others astray by a lack of knowledge? (See 1 Cor. 8.) Can one with limited knowledge be a leader?

Chapter Twelve

A HEALTHY HEART

And David shepherded them with integrity of heart;
with skillful hands he led them.

—PSALM 78:72

The best and most beautiful things in the world
cannot be seen or even touched.
They must be felt with the heart.

—HELEN KELLER

Your signature promise needs to be delivered with a healthy heart! Let me use another true story to explain. Mark Kirk was the newly appointed chief financial officer of Anchor Glass, Inc. He and the chief executive officer, Jim Malone, were flying from Europe back to the United States. The two men had just finished an exhausting weeklong "road show," selling investment securities. They traveled to Paris, London, and Zurich. In Switzerland, they decided to change plans and come home early. The ticket agent told Mr. Malone that both men could get on the plane. However, one seat was in first class and the other was in coach. Mr. Malone was older and the CEO. Mark was only twenty-eight years old at the time. He could sit easily in coach and properly so.

But that's not what happened.

After purchasing the tickets, Mr. Malone turned and handed the first class ticket to Mark. In deference, Mark refused to accept the ticket. Mr. Malone insisted that Mark take the ticket because Mark had never flown from Switzerland to the United States in first class. Mark recalls really enjoying the flight, eating shrimp and caviar while his boss was crammed in the back row of the airplane, near the stinky toilets, between two guys who used more than their fair share of seating.

Mark told me that Jim Malone's kindness that day caused Mark to be a forever-fan of Jim. Mark jumped through hoops, changed companies, changed cities, and worked relentlessly for this leader for many, many years because of the power of his boss's heart! As Mark says about his own employees, "you can buy a person's presence, a number of jobs per hour, a task to be done, but you cannot buy enthusiasm and the depths of their hearts." It must be earned.

----◦----

Beyond the power of knowledge, Jesus incessantly tapped the power of the heart. Heart power was central to his leadership. The heart is the human seat of affection and emotion. The power of the heart, therefore, influences human acts of kindness and compassion that touch the central nervous system of emotion in people's lives. The human heart helps people see God.[1] It helps people love God.[2] The heart reveals where your treasure is.[3] Things that affect us deeply are things of the heart.

Jesus used the power of the heart to open people up to his leadership and his teachable point of view. When Jesus healed and forgave the paralytic man, he touched more than flesh and blood. In the midst of a busy crowd, when the bleeding woman reached out to touch his cloak, Jesus healed her body *and* heart, saying, "Go in peace and be freed from your suffering."[4] He stopped amidst another crowd and showed compassion to a widow from Nain who had lost her only son to death. Jesus' "heart went out to her and he said, 'Don't cry.'"[5]

Would I have stopped? Would you have stopped? Probably not. Yet Christ stopped and healed them, in more ways than one. Jesus had compassion for them, taking time to notice them and touch them. When Jesus healed the blind, the lame, the deaf, and the crippled, he used the power of the heart by taking time to care. He touched the human seat of emotion in each of these cases by showing compassion and love.

The Jews were influenced by the power of the heart. When they saw Jesus "moved in spirit and troubled" over the death of Lazarus and the deep grief of Mary and Martha, they wanted to follow him. His compassion and empathy caused him to cry, and the Jews said, "see how he loved him!"[6] The heart of almighty God was so touched by human grief that hot tears coursed down Jesus' cheeks, and people followed. When the very heart of a leader breaks, the power of the heart is at work.

People followed Jesus because he cared about them. A brand of leadership that matters is a brand that values people. People follow people who care. Jesus always had a heart for people. When he saw the large crowds in Jerusalem he mourned, "O Jerusalem, Jerusalem, you who kill the prophets and stone those sent to you, how often I have longed to gather your children together, as a hen gathers her chicks under her wings, but you were not willing. Look, your house is left to you desolate."[7]

Jesus had tremendous compassion and kindness. He was a people person. He was for all people. He loved people. He cared for people. He served people. He healed people. He taught people. He died for people. People, people, people! He came to seek and save lost people! This domain of his power is, perhaps, the most compelling and influential because it touches the very heart and soul of mankind.

Watch how he works with his disciples just before the Passover feast. Jesus used heart power to influence his disciples at a critical time in his leadership. If I was calling the play, I think I might have used knowledge power in this instance, giving the disciples a motivational talk on leading change. Instead, Jesus uses the power of the heart at this moment in time. In fact,

> Jesus knew that the time had come for him to leave this world and go to the Father. Having loved his own who were in the world, he now showed them the full extent of his love. The evening meal was being served, and the devil had already prompted Judas Iscariot, son of Simon, to betray Jesus. Jesus knew the Father had put all things under his power, and that he had come from God and was returning to God; so he got up from the meal, took off his outer clothing, and wrapped a towel around his waist. After that, he poured water into a basin and began to wash his disciples' feet, drying them with the towel that was wrapped around him.[8]

Do you see the power of the heart coming through? Do you see how Jesus uses his power in combination? Jesus possessed all positional power and knowledge power. However, at this particular time, he used heart power in combination with the other powers to touch the inner souls and lives of those who were with him. He enhanced the play on the court of life that night by serving them. How could this be? Kings don't do this. Executives don't do this. But God always does this. Jesus' heart power reigns because he maintained a proper view of himself, a proper view of others, and a proper view of God. His father gave him power of the heart.

King David's brand of leadership stemmed from some strong heart power. In fact, God chose David to lead because of his heart power: "The LORD does not look at the things man looks at. Man looks at the outward appearance, but the LORD looks at the heart."[9] David, like Jesus, combined his *positional power* and his *knowledge power* with the power of the heart to be an effective leader. The masses wanted to follow David because he cared for the people under his watch.

The condition of David's mind was superb, but the tipping point in David's leadership appointment was the condition of his heart. When David lost this dimension of his leadership, he abused his positional power, taking Bathsheba, wife of Uriah the Hittite, to be his own wife.

To rebuke David,

The Lord sent Nathan to David. When he came to him, he said, "There were two men in a certain town, one rich and the other poor. The rich man had a very large number of sheep and cattle, but the poor man had nothing except one little ewe lamb he had bought. He raised it, and it grew up with him and his children. It shared his food, drank from his cup and even slept in his arms. It was like a daughter to him.

"Now a traveler came to the rich man, but the rich man refrained from taking one of his own sheep or cattle to prepare a meal for the traveler who had come to him. Instead, he took the ewe lamb that belonged to the poor man and prepared it for the one who had come to him."

David burned with anger against the man and said to Nathan, "As surely as the Lord lives, the man who did this deserves to die! He must pay for that lamb four times over, because he did such a thing and had no pity."

Then Nathan said to David, "You are the man! This is what the Lord, the God of Israel, says: 'I anointed you king over Israel, and I delivered you from the hand of Saul. I gave your master's house to you, and your master's wives into your arms. I gave you the house of Israel and Judah. And if all this had been too little, I would have given you even more. Why did you despise the word of the Lord by doing what is evil in his eyes? You struck down Uriah the Hittite with the sword and took his wife to be your own. You killed him with the sword of the Ammonites. Now, therefore, the sword will never depart from your house, because you despised me and took the wife of Uriah the Hittite to be your own.' This is what the Lord says: 'Out of your own household I am going to bring calamity upon you. Before your very eyes I will take your wives and give them to one who is close to you, and he will lie with your wives in broad daylight. You did it in secret, but I will do this thing in broad daylight before all Israel.'"[10]

Whoa! David lost so much because of his adulterous behavior, empty of heart. He did not use heart power when he should have.

The same thing happens today. Our leadership suffers when we lose power of the heart. It happens in our homes. We lose our overall influence over our children and our spouses when we lose the power of the heart. When we no longer have tender hearts, we close the spirits of those around us. It happens in our churches, too. Sometimes we are confident in our own knowledge of the scriptures, our own position of salvation, and our own righteousness. When this happens, the heart of the church hardens and loses power to do God's work.

The good news is that the great physician is at the top of his game when he encounters heart problems. "For the eyes of the Lord range throughout the earth to strengthen those whose hearts are fully committed to him."[11]

You can lose your knowledge power as you grow older and still lead distinctively with power of the heart. When you retire from recognized positions of power, you can still make a difference in your remaining positions with the power of the heart. However, if you become hardened to people's needs around you, no amount of knowledge and position can endear people to you. A brand of leadership with lasting power and influence results only when power of the heart is central and operational. When there is heart failure, there is true power failure.

Noted business authors acknowledge power of the heart and its role in leadership. Daniel Goleman, author of the bestselling book *Emotional Intelligence,* suggests that emotions, compassion, and the power of the heart are particularly central to leadership. He argues that distinctive leaders must possess intellectual ability combined with emotional intelligence and empathy. His research continues to suggest that the nature of one's heart becomes a powerful and defining characteristic of great leaders.[12]

In my own life, I have witnessed the influence of heart power. First, when I was a little boy, my mom and dad attended every one of my band concert performances. At first, that may seem quite normal to you. However, if you remember, my parents are deaf. They can't hear anything. (Some at the concert considered this a great blessing for my parents.) Regardless, for every band concert, they cheered me on even though it brought them no auditory pleasure. Those acts of kindness and support demonstrated a measure of their love that underpins my being to this day.

Second, my mom made the significant choice to stay home and raise me and my brothers. Our income was limited as a result. However, I will never trade the time and the relationship I developed with her because of her choice. When I entered college, she took a job as a cleaning woman, cleaning sinks and urinals in some of Michigan's restaurants to send me to college. I remember her excitement at times when she would come home showing us how much money she had found in the men's bathrooms that day! I think her largest single find was a twenty dollar bill. My life will never be the same because she showed me power of her heart.

Finally, many years ago, my dad learned that with surgery there was a possibility he could once again hear. After a series of tests on both him and mom, they consulted the doctor to review the results. The doctor shared the news that they thought a new surgical procedure could possibly restore Dad's hearing. Dad's first question for the doctor was, "What about Lois? Will Lois be able to hear?" "No," the doctor said. "She will never be able to hear because her nerves are dead." Dad pondered the situation and chose to refuse the operation, remaining deaf alongside my mom until his death.

My dad never held positions of great prestige at Ford Motor Company. He was never an executive. He never received a college education. My mom was never a successful career woman. She was never associated with people of great influence. She only completed the eighth grade. Neither of my parents ever had much knowledge power. But through the power of the heart, they built a brand of leadership that mattered and have provided distinctive leadership over me and shaped my life for an eternity!

Key Points

1. Not only did Jesus harness the power of position and knowledge, he tapped the power of the heart and it was central to his leadership.
2. Distinctive leaders have intellectual ability but it is always combined with emotional intelligence, empathy, and a heart that understands the deepest needs of people.
3. According to Psalm 78:72, King David led with both integrity of heart and skillful hands.
4. King David lost his heart power and found public disgrace to be his.
5. Jesus' heart was given to people. He was a people person. He was for all people.
6. Knowledge power and positional power are extremely effective. Heart power provides joy and healing along the way.
7. Regardless of age, income, social standing, knowledge, or occupation, God strengthens and uses hearts fully committed to him (2 Chron. 16:9).

Challenge

Remember, Vince Lombardi said, "you've got to be smart to be number one in any business. But more important, you've got to play with your heart—with every fiber of your body." It's true. It takes both mind and heart to achieve greatness.

The biggest killer in the U.S. is heart disease. For humans, it often seems the heart, physically and spiritually, is the most difficult to condition and maintain. Perhaps information and knowledge are more easily gained than real, costly love. The greater people's knowledge, the more likely they are to become puffed up or boastful, thinking too highly or too often about their own levels of accomplishment relative to others. This selfish perspective leads to heart disease of the worst kind. As mentioned earlier, the only way to a healthy heart is to (1) gain and maintain a proper perspective before God, (2) embrace a proper view of others, and (3) develop a spirit of obedience to God. I continue to believe one major reason for Jesus' birth in a feeding trough was to help him maintain a healthy perspective for his work on earth. It would be quite a stretch to brag about yourself knowing the reality of your beginning.

David evidently forgot about his start. It seems his daily digestion of success, accomplishment, and human fulfillment led to clogged arteries. When

Nathan rebuked David, he reminded him of who gave him success. Nathan said, "This is what the Lord, the God of Israel, says: 'I anointed you king over Israel, and I delivered you from the hand of Saul. I gave your master's house to you, and your master's wives into your arms. I gave you the house of Israel and Judah. And if all this had been too little, I would have given you even more.'"[13]

Throughout history, many have succumbed to heart disease. Cleansing oneself of a lofty personal perspective seems to be the only way to a heart-healthy lifestyle. All people come to the foot of the cross on equal ground, no matter their personal histories! A big challenge for building a leadership brand that matters will be to maintain a lifestyle that basks in the light of God, finding cleansing and perspective in his presence.

Exploring Big Ideas

1. Why is it so difficult to maintain a healthy heart?

2. Give some examples of distinctive leaders you know who seem to maintain a healthy heart. Can you gain perspective by analyzing and discussing what you know about their lifestyles?

3. Interview a distinctive leader with a healthy heart. Ask that person questions that probe how to maintain a heart-healthy lifestyle.

4. How did Jesus condition his heart? Can you list some exercises in which he regularly engaged to maintain and strengthen the condition of his heart?

5. How did Jesus use both the mind and the heart in combination to lead? Can you cite some examples where he used both, creating distinctive leadership moments?

6. List all the things about Jesus' heart that resulted in greatness.

7. What are the leading causes of heart disease in leaders today?

Chapter Thirteen

MORAL CHARACTER, EDGE, AND FAITH

When they saw the courage of Peter and John
and realized that they were unschooled,
ordinary men, they were astonished and
they took note that these men had been with Jesus.

—ACTS 4:13

Courage is being scared to death— but saddling up anyway.

—JOHN WAYNE

The final components of the promise are moral character, edge, and faith: a distinctive combination of that which makes you uniquely branded by God. Highlighting the notion that great leaders are persons of great character, the honorable James Baker III, sixty-first U.S. Secretary of State, told a group of Michigan business students, "There is no substitute for electing men and women of character and integrity to our boards and executive suites."[1] He continued, "Our founders understood that public virtue was absolutely essential— 'Of all the dispositions and habits which lead to political prosperity,' George Washington said in his Farewell Address, 'religion and morality are indispensable supports.'"[2]

Mr. Baker recounted America's strong desire for integrity in the White House after Watergate: "people demanded higher standards. And, we had four presidents in a row with the very highest character. President Gerald Ford was one of the finest men to ever serve as president. He restored honor to the Oval

Office. Jimmy Carter, in my view, was wrong on many policies and perhaps less skilled at governance, but nobody would ever question his honesty. I certainly never would. And Ronald Reagan and George H. W. Bush were both men of the highest integrity."[3]

Virtually every leadership survey points to honesty and integrity as key characteristics in admired leaders more often than any other leadership trait. For nearly thirty years, the notable research of Kouzes and Posner suggests that honesty continues to be the dominant characteristic in admired leaders. It is the number one characteristic cited since they began their research, and more than eighty-eight percent of their respondents name it as a key ingredient to successful leadership.

Their findings are consistently reinforced by the work of Korn/Ferry International, the highly respected and successful search firm, and the Columbia University Graduate School of Business. These organizations continuously survey top executives across the world (across North America, Latin America, Western Europe, and Asia). One of their joint surveys reports that "ethics are rated most highly among the personal characteristics needed by the ideal CEO." Also, respondents expected their chief executive to be "above reproach."[4]

My own research supports these studies, as well. In my latest survey of more than three hundred church leaders, the number one "key ingredient" of leadership named was honesty, followed by vision, patience, humility, and kindness. It is clear that those willing to follow someone into battle, the boardroom, the classroom, or the family room want to be assured that their leader is a person worthy of trust.

In the 2004 U.S. presidential election, many constituents were dumbfounded to learn that moral values and issues of integrity were the deciding factor in giving the presidency to George W. Bush by more than 3.5 million votes. Time and again, voters state that beliefs, personal integrity, and moral character do matter! They mattered then. They matter now. In 1860, the moniker "honest Abe" was used as a major component of the Republican campaign. Abraham Lincoln's reputation for honesty and integrity has endured. Without question, honesty is one of the major qualities that made him a great leader.[5]

On Wall Street, issues of personal integrity and moral character are front-page news. The latest wave of scandals has revealed a very clear message about integrity. It seems that executives at AIG, Dynegy, Enron, Merrill Lynch,

WorldCom, Tyco, and the now famous Bernie Madoff, who have been involved in financial fraud, are more likely to have been involved in fraud in other areas of their lives, as well. For example, Nathan Chapman was sentenced to seven and a half years in prison for defrauding Maryland's state pension fund system and for looting his three publicly traded companies—and it was the testimonies of three former mistresses that helped put him behind bars.

One national article entitled "Business scandals prompt look into personal lives: Some executives facing legal trouble also hit marital rocks" notes that investigators are finding "a common thread running through some of the recent scandal-prone companies: many top executives accused of betraying the trust of shareholders also betrayed the trust of their wives."[6]

For example, former Tyco CEO Dennis Kozlowski had at least two affairs with subordinates before he divorced his first wife and married his mistress, according to trial testimony. WorldCom's Bernie Ebbers openly courted a company sales executive while married to his first wife. Enron's Jeff Skilling, who said he left the company in 2001 to tend to "family matters," divorced his wife four years earlier, taking up residence with a coworker nicknamed "VaVoom." Meanwhile two other top Enron officials were openly dating women—one a stripper and the other a coworker—outside of their marriages, according to former colleagues.[7]

The threads of fraud and infidelity is being found in the tapestry of these criminals' lives. According to Thomas DiBiagio, U.S. attorney for the state of Maryland, "prosecutors investigate cases using 'instincts and common sense' and recognize the traits philanderers and white-collar criminals might share. If their life is a lie, it's not confined to their personal life,' says DiBiagio. 'If they are lying to their wives, there's a huge potential they are also lying to their colleagues, their board of directors and potentially their auditors.'"[8]

Moral character, or the lack thereof, permeates all aspects of an individual's life. The presence of moral character is extremely powerful, in part because it creates trust between the leader and all followers. Trust produces distinctive leadership, but leadership without trust is dead. If you are dishonest, you will never hold enduring power nor rise to a level of leadership that matters! You certainly won't carry the brand of God.

Daniel abandoned the ordinary, making moral character part of his distinctive promise. The Old Testament testifies that Daniel was appointed to significant positions of leadership in three different Babylonian administrations, beginning with that of King Nebuchadnezzar, because he distinguished himself as a man of moral character. In fact, though the government officials tried to find flaws in his conduct, "they could find no corruption in him, because he was trustworthy and neither corrupt nor negligent."[9] He refused to eat and drink food from the table of the king, knowing that God had commanded him not to eat food offered to idols. He prayed to God three times a day, even when the law forbade him. In short, he lived a clean life in the midst of a corrupt society. His moral character was extraordinary not ordinary! He was distinctive—he had God's brand.

Daniel was consistent. His character was informed and formed from the inside out. Like a seaworthy vessel, Daniel had more weight below the waterline than he did above it. That is why he never capsized. His character was the result of a long process of faith and obedience to God.

With his impeccable character, Daniel was not interested in gaining credentials and prominence. Rather, he was interested in what God might do with his life. He believed God had placed him in three separate administrations in Babylon for a reason: to proclaim God's glory! As such, Daniel lived his personal and private faith in a very public way. According to James, we are all to be like that—Christians of character, so that we might be a kind of "firstfruits" of all that he created, showing God's glory in the way we live and showing what is yet to come from the people of God.[10]

Joseph is another example of outstanding and distinctive moral character. He, too, lived clean in the midst of a corrupt society, demonstrating the power of God's brand. Joseph forfeited his freedom rather than compromise his convictions. He rose to a top position in Egypt because he was trustworthy, a faithful steward of all Potiphar's possessions, including his wife who continually delivered sultry pleas for him to sleep with her. He resisted. He lived clean. He abandoned the ordinary, maintaining self control because he knew generic living and leading would not impact his culture for God.

The Bible says, the Lord was with him and he was blessed by God. However, Joseph's moral character came with a cost. He angered the wife of Potiphar by refusing her. Thus, she wrongly accused Joseph and had him imprisoned. Though imprisoned, he did not defend himself. He simply committed himself to godliness. His character and commitment came at a cost to him in the short run. However, in the long run, his character proved, again, to move him toward greatness. Joseph knew God's tests were meant for good, learning that God is not in the business of solving all problems but instead in the business of developing his person for his purposes.

As seen in the accounts of Joseph and Daniel, the personal characteristic of integrity, according to Stephen Carter, Yale University Law professor, consists of three basic ingredients: (1) the ability to discern right from wrong, (2) the ability to reason and articulate your conclusions about what is right and wrong, and (3) the willingness to stand up for your beliefs, regardless of the personal consequences. Each of these godly leaders demonstrated competence in each of these areas, abandoning the ordinary and displaying integrity in leadership for all generations.

One of my other leadership heroes is Andy Griffith. His humility, honesty, wisdom, and human compassion make him a great fictional leader to emulate. In one famous episode, Andy messes up. He becomes entrapped in a series of lies. While trying to sell an old city cannon to a junk dealer passing through Mayberry, Andy makes up stories about how the cannon was used by Teddy Roosevelt and his troops. Barney, Ellen, and Opie witness Andy's dishonesty and lose faith in him as their leader. When confronted, he explains he's just doing a little "horse-trading." They say he is lying. His breech of character causes Opie, his son, to follow suit and trade a pair of old cuff links for a brand new bicycle, claiming the cuff links were worn by General George Washington.

Andy finally realizes the error of his ways and sees that his dishonesty is leading his son and friends away from the type of honest living he continually espouses. He comes clean. He tells the truth and apologizes to everyone, restoring the integrity of his leadership. Andy had always been known for his integrity and honest approach as the city leader. But, with one slip, he discouraged and disenfranchised all of his trusted followers. It is the same with you and me.

We always tell our girls, everyone is watching you. Your friends are watching you. Our friends are watching you. My students are watching you. And thousands of others are watching you each day. You have the opportunity each day to deliver on the promises of God and be a strong moral example to others through your behavior. Keep your promises. Always tell the truth. Do right by people. Be discerning. Be a leader with distinction.

I nearly engaged in some "horse-trading" of my own a few years ago when shopping for a new family video camera. Jeanne and I quickly realized we had a significant dilemma on our hands. If we purchased a new digital camera, we would have no way of viewing our vast collection of 8mm family tapes that contained the history of our family life since the girls were born. As the sales clerk overheard us discussing our situation, he offered a suggestion. Motioning for us to come closer, he whispered, "Why don't you just buy this 'low-end' digital recorder, take it home, transfer all your old 8mm movies to digital format, then bring the recorder back within two weeks and say you don't want it? The store will take it back if you keep your receipt."

I thought to myself, "This is creative, though extremely dishonest." I explained to the young man the inappropriate nature of his big idea, especially as a representative of Circuit City. (Perhaps this is part of why Circuit City went bankrupt.) He looked a bit confused. Clearly, what he suggested to us was not registering in his mind as "wrong." As we continued our conversation, he looked more closely at us and said, "Hey. Aren't you the dean of the school of business at ACU?" "Yes I am," I replied. With a smile he said, "I'm one of your students. I'm a management major in the College of Business," displaying again the lack of connection between his dishonest suggestion and his personal brand of leadership. "Oh great!" I thought. In dismay, I dropped my head, looked at Jeanne and said, "We have a lot of work to do!"

As we left, I reflected on how easily I could have agreed to the young man's scheme. In an undisciplined moment, I could have given in! My student would have witnessed the dean of the College of Business at Abilene Christian University making a dishonest choice. I would have undermined the brand, becoming generic, common, like all others. As is often said, credibility and trust are built over a lifetime and often destroyed in a moment.

Consider the quick descent and destruction resulting from the lack of integrity in so many notable U.S. athletes. Michael Phelps, eight-time winner of Olympic Gold in the 2008 Beijing games, Alex Rodriguez, former Texas Rangers hero and New York Yankees baseball great, Marion Jones, five-time Olympic medalist in the 2004 games, Barry Bonds, home run king for the San Francisco Giants, and Jason Giami, New York Yankees slugger—all have been incriminated for lack of integrity regarding performance enhancing drugs. Tiger Woods, through numerous indiscretions, destroyed the most valuable brand in the history of golf. Due to lack of integrity, the distinction of these athletes eroded, their endorsements on cereal boxes forever withdrawn and their names dishonored. I am certain these gifted athletes did not plan to become fraudulent persons. However, the lure of better performance, the power of their status, just like their counterparts in business, caused them to breach their integrity while simultaneously and publicly denying the allegations.

George W. Bush in his 2004 State of the Union address stated, "Athletics play such an important role in our society, but, unfortunately, some in professional sports are not setting much of an example. The use of performance enhancing drugs like steroids in baseball, football, and other sports is dangerous, and it sends the wrong message—that there are shortcuts to accomplishment, and that performance is more important than character."[11]

In contrast, consider the name Garth Pleasant. He is not a noted U.S. athlete or coach. However, his name is synonymous with moral character and distinctive leadership for hundreds of athletes over the last thirty years in Michigan basketball. Coach Pleasant is one of only three collegiate basketball coaches to have accumulated more than five hundred wins in the history of Michigan basketball. All of these wins have occurred during his tenure as men's basketball coach at a small private Christian college—Rochester College, Rochester Hills, Michigan. During his career, he made six "final four" appearances, five championship appearances, and won one national title. He has earned numerous coach-of-the-year awards and influenced the lives of hundreds of young people. How did he do it? The power of his character!

Though many people say many things about him, they all point to his moral character as the transforming element in his coaching. One of his players said of him, "He has dealt with kids from every aspect of life. His influence spans from the inner city to the suburbs. There is no type of athlete that Coach Pleasant has not reached. There is no group of people that he has not transformed. Everything he touches is consumed by his character. Coach has never cheated. He has never smoothed over an ACT score. He has turned away Division I athletes because they would contradict the spirit of the school. He has never used a player merely to get wins. He has always held their spiritual life and academic degree in higher esteem than their points-per-game statistics. He is a man who ends practice with the following simple words, "Men, I love to win. I hope we win twenty games this year. But I'd rather go 0–20 and see all of you in heaven, more than I desire a win, a good season, or even a championship." In the words of one player, "For that reason, I will always call him Coach."[12]

As a follower of Jesus, I can say that his moral character is one of the reasons I will always call him Lord. I believe his word to be true. The truth of an individual's word was included in Jesus' teachable point of view on the mountainside. In the midst of his sermon he said, "Again, you have heard that it was said to the people long ago, 'Do not break your oath, but keep the oaths you have made to the Lord.' But I tell you, Do not swear at all: either by heaven, for it is God's throne; or by the earth, for it is his footstool; or by Jerusalem, for it is the city of the Great King. And do not swear by your head, for you cannot make even one hair white or black. Simply let your 'Yes' be 'Yes' and your 'No,' 'No.'; anything beyond this comes from the evil one."[13] The lesson: your word is to be truth. It should be held in high honor by you and those who follow you.

Jesus proclaimed to his followers, "I tell you the truth . . . I tell you the truth . . . I tell you the truth . . . ." More than eighty times in the New Testament, it is recorded that Jesus used this terminology, underscoring the importance of his word. His word among his disciples is without question. Therefore, millions continue to follow his leadership until he comes again! He told us he would. He gave us his word! The apostles followed Jesus' lead and emphasized the importance of truth in leadership. They taught that elders and deacons should be men above reproach, worthy of respect, holding to the deep truths with which they have been entrusted. They are to be blameless, not seekers of dishonest gain, holding firmly to the trustworthy message as it has been taught, encouraging others by sound doctrine.[14]

Moral leaders build high levels of trust among their followers, holding tremendous power and influence over them because the power of moral character is from above. The power of truth sets people free to follow by choice. Without truth, the power of leadership is relegated back to the realm of coercion, where people only follow because they have no options. Jesus said, when you know the truth, it will set you free.[15]

Edge

"Edge" is the ability to make tough decisions, and it distinctively marks a godly leader. Simple decision-making is akin to paddling a raft in calm water. Each decision, in and of itself, is relatively unimportant and normally goes unchallenged;

like a single paddle stroke, it can easily be corrected. However, tough decision-making is akin to paddling a raft while shooting the rapids in white water. In those situations, each decision is extremely important, and the group is looking for a leader they trust to make the calls.

Those in the raft may be fearful, questioning some decisions, but they will generally comply under stress. You might want to be prepared, because you can be sure they will offer a variety of opinions once through the rapids. When this happens, remember, the masses will always have opinions, but distinctive leaders make decisions.

Demonstrating edge may be a leader's most difficult power proposition. Edge requires courage and conviction. It requires keen insight. It requires wisdom and judgment. And, it is often painful. A leader with edge is willing to say "no" or "yes" in a given situation. "Edgy" leaders ensure that decisions align with their personal values and the ideas and values of their organizations. A leader without edge will find a way to avoid the inherent conflict, deciding it is something to be lived with. When the rest of the group or organization sees that a leader's actions don't add up, that leader's influence plummets.[16]

Jack Welch is often referred to as Neutron Jack because he had edge. Though Welch is a formidable competitor and many disliked him, I believe his edge was aligned with the vision and values of GE. His tough decisions supported the vision of the company. I remember listening to him explain why he always let the bottom twenty percent of his workforce go. Many people criticized him, saying he had no kindness. Welch replied that it is not kind to lie to people about their performance. Kindness tells the truth. Kindness informs the person that their work practices and habits do not align with the agreed-upon goals of the organization. Indeed, kindness may provide a wake-up call early in a person's career so they are able to make changes and develop a better track record down the road.

Edge does not listen to the voice of the crowd. When a leader seeks popularity among people, he or she has no edge. Respected leaders have edge. I remember the first time I had to make a decision to let an employee go. I exhausted myself over the decision. However, once I made the decision, the rest of the team responded with respect because they knew it was the right decision. If I would have "just let her play," I would have abused my positional power. Distinctive leaders must accept responsibility for making the tough decisions that need to be made for the good of the organization.

Ronald Reagan once said, "If you want to get to the other side of a wave, you must first swim toward it." In other words, if you want to get to a place of peace on the other side of a difficult decision, face the tough decision, move toward it, deal with it, and get on with it. Many times, I think Christian leaders fail here. They don't seem to have the edge necessary to make tough decisions. I am most surprised that many Christian parents have no leadership edge with their children. At times, I see spouses who don't have any edge with each other. I don't fully understand how our Christian faith seems to correlate to weakness in this area, but I believe it has something to do with misunderstandings of passages that call for us to be kind, meek, and humble.

For Jesus, edge was a function of his tender toughness. It is two-sided. It defined his brand of leadership. It is neither all one nor the other, but both. It is like the word of God: Jesus himself. "For the word of God is living and active. Sharper than any double-edged sword, it penetrates even to dividing soul and spirit, joints and marrow; it judges the thoughts and attitudes of the heart."[17] The apostle Paul speaks of the balanced edge of God in decision-making regarding reconciliation when he says, "consider therefore the kindness and the sternness of God."[18]

The key, therefore, to leadership edge is in knowing when to deploy which side of the blade. To gain perspective, let's consider the edge of Jesus. First, let's consider his tenderness. This won't take long, since we reviewed Jesus' heart-healthy lifestyle in the previous chapter. Clearly, Jesus used power of the heart in his leadership. Jesus treated people tenderly with compassion, caring, and kindness. He showed tenderness to many, including adulterers, the blind, the deaf, and the crippled. At the end of his life, he dramatically showed great compassion and mercy to the thief hanging on the cross next to him.

Now, let's consider the toughness of Jesus. As the Dodge Ram Truck advertisement used to say, "If it was any tougher, it would have made its own license plates." Jesus was that tough! He fought with the best of them and asked his followers to be tough as well! The toughness we are referring to is the other side of the double-edged sword. It is the edge needed to make difficult and unpopular decisions when they are needed. John the Baptist displayed some nice edge when he told Herod that he shouldn't sleep with his brother's wife. John was locked up in prison and eventually lost his head. Following suit, Jesus displayed some notable edge when he cleared the temple, overturning the tables of the money changers and driving them out because they had turned his father's house into a corrupt market.

Jesus spoke with edge on many occasions. He told a group of Jews that their father was the devil: a murderer and liar from the beginning.[19] He told the Pharisees they were hypocrites, (1) binding up burdens on men without lifting a finger to help, (2) loving to be greeted in the streets for their fancy prayers, (3) exalting themselves in front of others, (4) leading converts astray through their own wicked practices, (5) swearing by the temple without regard for its sacred nature, (6) having no mercy while following strict rules of giving, and (7) appearing righteous but being full of dead men's bones on the inside.[20]

It was Jesus who spoke about hell. Talk about edge! The Greek word for hell is found only twelve times in the New Testament. Eleven of those twelve times, it is found on the lips of Jesus. The only other time it is used by James, Jesus' brother. Jesus also spoke with edge when he taught the parable of the talents. I'm sure it was not easy to tell people that if they didn't secure a positive return for what they had been given, everything they had would be taken away from them. Ouch! Neutron Jesus! His teaching had edge. Consider his teachings about the narrow door, the cost of being a disciple, the shrewd manager, the rich man and Lazarus, the rich young ruler, or the ten virgins. These are "edgy!" It would have been easier to gloss over the truth and seek popularity in his leadership. But Jesus always taught and treated people in a way that aligned with his mission and values. He had godly edge.

Those who abandon ordinary leadership build distinctive brands by knowing how and when to use each side of the sword. They properly assess each situation, consider their personal mission and values, consider the mission and values of those involved, and make tough decisions to move people forward. These decisions are more art than science. Primarily the judgment has to deal with the situation at hand and the heart of the people involved. This means choosing the appropriate side of the sword is never easy!

Let's look at a few more examples from the life of Jesus to see how he used edge. Let's begin at the end. At the end of Jesus' ministry, before he is to ascend back to heaven, he highlights the nature of his positional power, telling the disciples that he has all authority and power in heaven and earth. He tells them to go forth proclaiming his power to all nations. Why did Jesus use positional power in this situation instead of power of the heart? I think because Jesus knew that the disciples needed to be assured that he had the positional power to do what he was asking them to do. They didn't need him to cry with them. They needed assurance they could accomplish the mission.

At the cross, Jesus' positional power ultimately had to be utilized to provide leadership that purchased salvation for the rest of us. The thoughts of his heart and all of his knowledge would not ultimately get the job done. He eventually had to get on the cross. He could not have calmed the storm with stories. He didn't need to explain to the disciples that he had all knowledge about the storm. He didn't need to cry with them because they were afraid. He could only calm the storm by his positional power over physical and spiritual forces. Similarly, Jesus used his positional power to drive out evil spirits. He was God and had dominion over Satan, thus he was able to drive the demons out of people. People who were possessed by evil needed Jesus to summon the power of his position to help them. Crying for them would have been nice, but tears would not have accomplished the task. He was put in charge, so he took charge!

On the mountains, Jesus often used his knowledge to lead the people. Normally, the masses did not need Jesus to cry with them, nor did they need him to enact his positional power over them. Instead, in his sermon on the mount, he shared his teachable point of view with his followers because they needed to understand what he was all about. They needed information and knowledge to help them live their lives. They needed to know what to do to be saved. They needed to understand what judgment would be like. They needed to learn about hell. Every person listening was curious to know about God and how God interacted with people. Jesus often told the Pharisees they were in error because they did not know the scriptures and the power of God.[21] Thus, he taught them and shared his knowledge with them. It was during these times that his knowledge provided powerful leadership over the people when they were lost and helpless, like sheep without a shepherd.

The tenderness of Jesus, his heart power, was used when he encountered the man with leprosy, the paralytic, the sinful woman, a dead girl, a sick woman, the four thousand, Mary and Martha, the crippled woman, the twelve at the last supper, and others. These individuals did not need a lecture on why these things had happened. They did not need a speech about Jesus' positional power to be able to heal. They needed the balm of Gilead: his sympathy, tenderness, and concern for their situation.

In summary, a consistent scriptural framework emerges for determining which edge of the sword to use in a given leadership setting. Use the tender edge of the sword when the people you are leading have broken hearts. Broken hearts need healing, not hammering. At other times, when you encounter hypocrisy, the voice of the crowd, and the opponent, use the tough edge of the sword. Jesus was tough on hypocrisy because it is duplicity of heart and mind that is contrary to truth. He hammered hypocrisy, the voice of the crowd, and the devil with the cutting edge of truth and positional power (all authority).

Jesus consistently used positional power if people needed a savior to rescue them from sin. He used knowledge power when people were confused and misinformed or evil. He used heart power when people needed assurance, sympathy, and salve for a broken condition. Regardless, Jesus always told the truth, and it was always seasoned with grace in its proper sword form. In every situation, Jesus discerned which type of power was needed and used it appropriately in a given scenario.

The "edge" of Jesus delivers high marks on the court of life. It is a powerful leadership framework capable of moving you away from generic toward a distinctive brand of leadership that matters!

Faith Power

In the end—when everyone else deserted him—when it was time for the rubber to meet the road—it was Jesus' faith that empowered him to complete his distinctive leadership journey. Faith took him to the temple, to the marketplace, to the mountains, and to the sea. Faith drove him to a night-long prayer vigil in a lonely garden. Faith caused the Son of God to dip his bread in a common bowl with a traitor named Iscariot. The road to the cross was paved with faith.

When leaders believe the God of Abraham, Isaac, and Jacob is able to do immeasurably more than they could possibly ask or imagine according to his power at work within them, they unleash the power of faith.[22] Faithful leadership is the assurance of what is hoped for and the certainty of what is not seen.[23] It is being fully persuaded that God has power to do what he has promised.[24] Ultimately, it is the sentiment of Mary, the mother of Jesus, who said, "I am the Lord's servant. May it be to me as you have said."[25] As such, it is the most ethereal and elusive yet significant type of power. It is, indeed, a mystery. It does not reside on the pages of most leadership textbooks as a source of power. But it resides on the pages of history as the ultimate source of power to do the distinctive work of God!

Faith gives leaders the power to drive change. Faith gives courage. It provides energy and commitment to the task. Faith results in determination. Faith gets the job done. Faith drives obedience. By faith we all understand that the universe was formed at God's command.[26] Noah, in holy fear, built an ark by faith to save his family, and he became heir of the righteousness that comes by faith.[27] By faith, Abraham obeyed and led the people of God, leaving his home country even though he did not know where he was going. Eventually, he became a father because he considered God faithful who had made the promise. Once the promise was fulfilled, he offered his only son of the promise, Isaac, back to God.[28]

My hero, Moses, began his leadership journey on the coattails of his mother's faith. His mother hid him for three months because she had faith and saw that he was no ordinary child. The Red Sea was crossed by faith. The walls of Jericho came down by faith. Rahab the prostitute hid the spies by faith. Gideon, Barak, Deborah, Samson, David, Samuel, Esther, and the prophets all provided great leadership through incredible faith. Other great women, by faith, received back their dead. Many more were tortured, flogged, stoned, and imprisoned by faith.

In our own national history, faith is found at the center of our struggle in World War II. Tom Brokaw, in his book *The Greatest Generation*, articulates how faith and deeply held spiritual beliefs of young men and women who went off to war "helped them cope with the constant presence of possible death, serious injury, or the other anxieties attendant to the disruptions brought on by war."[29] "I think we were on God's side," says the Reverend Harry Reginald Hammond. "The United States has done some foolish things, but in that war I knew we had God with us. It made me realize that there was something much larger than just me. I realized it had to be God."[30] Others like Helen Van Gorder used their faith to help them through the challenges of war: "Faith helped her through the great strains of having a husband, and later a son, in the line of fire. Faith was the twin to love in the marriage of the Brodericks, another heroic couple of that generation."[31]

Faith helps leaders overcome two inherent challenges to abandoning the ordinary and building a brand of distinctive leadership that matters: failure and opposition. These two are ferocious adversaries, coming to visit all leaders in time. Without faith, all would be overcome by their power.

Faith Challenge No. 1: Failure. Leaders fail. They become discouraged, beginning to believe the tenets of failure rather than the promises of God. Failure and discouragement attack time and again, depleting the very soul which calls them to lead. Fatigue befalls them and, as coach Lombardi said, "makes cowards of us all!" It is true. However, failure, exhaustion, and discouragement do not have to be final! Henry Ford went bankrupt in his first year in the automobile business, and two years later his second company failed. Through faith and determination, his third company is recording a string of successes and is currently, as of 2010, the strongest of the Detroit Big Three. Ronald Reagan failed at his first two attempts to win the White House but Reagan's faith pushed him toward a rendezvous with destiny; so, he ran again! Michael Jordan was cut from his high school basketball team as a sophomore. For most people, that would have marked the end of a basketball career. But Michael's dream and his faith in that dream kept him working until he became one of the greatest basketball players who ever lived.

The apostle Paul failed in his first effort to evangelize the Middle East, and he had to flee Damascus under the cover of night.[32] He had to back up and try again. His faith allowed him to persist until he flooded the entire Roman Empire with the gospel of Jesus Christ. Douglas MacArthur, one of the world's noted military leaders, dreamed of going to West Point military academy. He was turned down twice. He persisted, applied a third time and was accepted. The rest is history. Twenty-three publishers rejected a children's book written by an author who called himself Dr. Suess. The twenty-fourth publisher liked it. It sold six million copies.

Faith Challenge No. 2: Opposition. Leaders will always face opposition. People generally don't embrace change, especially if things appear to be going well. Only through faith can we really change who we are. People in darkness are miserable, but they don't want to face uncomfortable light. When a wheel turns it creates friction. The important thing to note is that the wheel is moving. Standing still, the wheel causes zero friction—but goes nowhere. The leader moves the wheel, friction results!

The late U.S. attorney general Robert Kennedy said, "Twenty percent of the people will be against anything." Thomas Jefferson noted, "Good people with good intentions and the same facts don't always agree."[33] How true. How true! When Moses attempted to lead the children of Israel out of bondage he faced continual criticism. He faced it from Pharoah. Then, he faced it from the Israelites, who complained about the plan, the process, the timing, and the results. He was criticized for his faith in God, his provision, his unwavering commitment, and his inability to settle their disputes. Without faith, Moses would have quit early in the process. In fact, as we have seen previously, Moses wanted to quit. However, his deep faith and reverence for God bound him to the task at hand. He did not give up!

Faith drives us to remember and embrace the famous words of Theodore Roosevelt:

> It's not the critic who counts, not the man who points out how the strong man stumbles or where the doer of deeds could have done them better. The credit belongs to the man who is actually in the arena; whose face is marred by the dust and sweat and blood; who strives valiantly; who errs and comes up short again and again; who knows the great enthusiasms, the great devotions, and spends himself in a worthy cause; who at the worst, if he fails, at least fails while daring greatly; so that his place shall never be with those cold and timid souls who know neither defeat nor victory.[34]

And the common man's teacher, Mark Twain, said "Every dog needs a few fleas. It helps him take his mind off being a dog." We need to be reminded that critics cannot distress you unless you allow them to do so. James L. Sullivan, former president of the Sunday School Board of the Southern Baptist Convention, said, "A Horse fly never hurt a thoroughbred unless he annoyed him into doing something crazy."[35]

In a teachable moment on the open sea in the midst of a storm, the disciples were fearful. Jesus challenged them saying, "Oh you of little faith."[36] The faith of a few good friends healed a discouraged paralytic and provided him forgiveness from sin.[37] A bleeding woman fought the crowds to touch the hem of Jesus' garment, finding her faith had healed her.[38] Two blind men pursued sight with Jesus. He said, "'Do you believe I am able to do this?' 'Yes, Lord, they replied.' He touched their eyes and said, 'According to your faith will it be done to you.'"[39]

Fundamental to a brand of distinctive leadership is active faith! Without faith, it is impossible to please God.[40] Faith is difficult, and it often fluctuates under the heavy pressures of life "on the court." All of us should take comfort in knowing that the apostles struggled with their faith. When told to forgive men seven times in a day, the apostles cried out "Increase our faith!"[41]

Seek faith and strength on this leadership journey. May you be blessed by a prayer of Eleanor Roosevelt I recently discovered in the home of Jack and Ann Griggs. It resonates deeply with me.

> Our father, who has set a restlessness in our hearts and made us all seekers after that which we can never fully find, keep us at tasks too hard for us, that we may be driven to thee for strength.

Amen!

Key Points

1. Moral character is the number one leadership trait sought by followers.
2. Honesty and integrity cannot be contained. If possessed, they permeate all aspects of life.
3. Fraud cannot be contained. It is a common thread running through all of life.
4. Edge requires keen insight, wisdom, and judgment. Without edge, leaders play to the masses.
5. Godly edge is two-sided. It is both tough and tender, given the needs of the people involved.
6. When the rubber met the road, faith enabled Jesus to complete his distinctive leadership journey. The supernatural can only be done by faith.
7. Finally, without faith, it is impossible to please God.

Challenge

Demonstrating moral character, edge, and faith may be the leader's most difficult power proposition. These tools require courage and conviction. They require keen insight. They require wisdom and judgment. They are often painful, but an individual who is not willing to say "no" or "yes" in a given situation, based on moral courage and faith, is not a leader branded by God. To the contrary, an "edgy" Christian leader ensures that all decisions align with God's will, his or her personal values, and the mission of the group being led. This edge must exist in the home, the church, the community, and the global marketplace.

As we discussed in Chapter One, generic living and leadership proves unattractive, holding little power to influence and create value for others. However, leaders whose lives reflect moral quality and distinction hold the power to create significant value and influence in others for change that really matters!

Remember, in the end—when everyone else deserted him—when it was time for the rubber to meet the road—it was the power of Jesus' moral character, edge, and faith that enabled him to complete his distinctive leadership journey. He built a brand of leadership that matters! His brand has the power to change you for eternity. It was his brand that took him to the temple. It was his brand that took him to the garden. It was his brand that made him dip his bread with

Judas. The road to the cross was cleared by his brand. The challenge before you is to build a brand that matters in the lives of those you love and lead.

Exploring Big Ideas

1. Describe why moral character is so important in leadership. Give a personal example of a time when a leader's moral character made a difference for you as a follower.

2. Why do you think moral character, or the lack thereof, cannot be compartmentalized? Must it permeate all areas of an individual's life?

3. Note some examples of leaders you know who use edge appropriately to influence and persuade others effectively.

4. Can you think of a time when a leader used toughness when tenderness was needed? Explain what resulted from the misjudgment.

5. How does faith cause one to build a leadership brand that matters? Can you give an example of a time when your faith helped you demonstrate distinction in your life?

6. How did Jesus use moral character, edge, and faith in combination to lead? Cite some examples in which he used each of these strategically, creating value in the lives of others.

7. Describe a time when failure, discouragement, or opposition caused you to lose faith, devaluing your brand of leadership.

A FINAL THOUGHT

All authority in heaven and on earth has been given to me.
Therefore, go and make disciples of all nations,
baptizing them in the name of the Father and of the Son
and of the Holy Spirit, and teaching them to obey everything
I have commanded you. And surely, I will be with you always,
to the very end of the age.

—MATTHEW 28:18–20

T he great commission is a daunting passage for many. It is for me. The task seems too great. It appears to be a little too all-encompassing. How can I be responsible for the whole world? Somehow it is a bit much for me to comprehend. Is it even possible? Jesus, come on. Be real.

Our response to this, the greatest of all Christian challenges, is a function of the power we have. To pull this off, we must have God's vision, his presence, his power, his attitude, his position, his knowledge, his heart, his character, his edge, and his faith. The job is too great for anything else. Nothing less will do.

As Moses cried out to God, what will make us distinctive from all other peoples on the face of the earth? God answers, Come see my glory! When you see my glory, you will be distinctive.

As limited as I am, my faith is in Jesus! I am banking everything I am and everything I hope to become as a leader on Jesus. What I do with my God-given positions on the court of life will be my leadership legacy. It will either be distinctive or ordinary. I pray for distinctive.

If you believe Jesus and claim to be in him, you must walk as he did.[1] Throughout Jesus' leadership journey, he used power to move people ahead in their lives. When he confronted all of the brokenness and confusion on the court where God had placed him, he always responded with the appropriate type of power people needed at the time. If someone needed the power of his position, he used it to provide leadership and dominion over them in order to get things done. He was in charge, so he took charge!

If people were without understanding, he used his knowledge power to help them grasp a perspective on their current reality. When he encountered those with broken hearts, no matter what the sin, he provided the power of the heart to touch their lives and restore order and healing. When he had to make tough calls, Jesus used truthful edge to deliver the message and do the right thing. When he struggled to complete the task he had been given, he dropped to his knees in faith, knowing this was the only type of power that would work, and cried out to his father in heaven for help.[2]

The wonder of this portrait of leadership is that we, too, can provide distinctive leadership with power through a brand that really matters if we follow the pattern of Jesus and are empowered by his purpose and the presence of God! First, we must seek the power of his perspective, having good eyes that fill our whole bodies full of light. Second, we must understand the power and responsibility of the positions we have been given. Next, we must find his power, having our souls branded with the mark of his glory. Finally, we must create and manage a signature brand of leadership—a set of promises signed by the very spirit of God—through our own gifts and positions.

When we contemplate distinctive leadership in our families, the formula is the same. When we attempt to abandon the ordinary and provide distinctive leadership for our churches, the formula is the same. At the office, it remains the same. In government, it doesn't waiver. This is a leadership formula that has worked throughout history.

The distinctive leader must remember that it is Jesus' positional power that brings salvation. When we fully understand his positional power, we fall down and worship him like the disciples in the storm on the Sea of Galilee. It is Jesus' knowledge power that provides us with the information and ideas we need to understand our reality and embrace a picture of hope for the future. But it is the power of the heart that opens up the souls of men and women, providing them the opportunity to follow our lead as we help them see the glory of God. As we undertake the task, may we each have the edge, integrity, and faith power necessary to allow God to work miraculously among us and within us as ambassadors for Christ on earth.

Don't forget this paramount truth—we each have access to the power of his presence, the power of his purpose, and the power of his brand, enabling us to be extraordinary leaders who can reach levels of greatness and leadership before unknown. It's the power of the cross and the Christ on the cross. It is salt power. It is light power. It is power that, when you embrace it in your positions of power, will change the world.

Eugene Peterson, author of *The Message*, compares and contrasts the leadership legacies of Jesus and Herod. His theme is "follow the leader." I think Peterson does a marvelous job of illustrating the power of Jesus' distinctive leadership compared with a seemingly powerful example of worldly leadership. Both Jesus and Herod were distinctive leaders. Only one was legendary.

From Peterson's work: "The leading leaders at the beginning of the Christian era were Jesus and Herod. It is interesting to observe what has happened in the 2,000 years since. Jesus is the name that continues to be recognized and honored.But, [Herod's name is] obscure and of interest only to historians . . . ." I am interested in that contrast and its implications. Jesus was born and Herod died in approximately the same year.

The contrast between Jesus' life and Herod's death could hardly be more stark. Jesus was born in a shelter for animals in Bethlehem. Probably a cave with a wide opening, which was a usual shelter for domestic animals—sheep and goats and cows in those years. Herod was buried in lavish pomp, carried in an extravagant funeral procession on a gold litter from Jericho to a mountain that he had created and named after himself: Herodian. There was a modest natural hill nearby but nothing approaching the size that Herod required so he had the mountain built higher and higher and higher, moving huge quantities of dirt and rock so that eventually it loomed huge over the desert horizon. And then his elaborate palace was constructed on the pinnacle which is still a stunning piece of architecture, breathtakingly elegant.

Herod's burial mountain is about three miles from Jesus' birth cave. Jesus' birth was a quiet affair out of the way, affectionately attended by his parents, a few young shepherds, some visiting religious scholars, a donkey and a cow or two. Herod's burial was neither obscure nor quiet nor affectionate, and he didn't plan to disappear into the grave forgotten when he died. This was an in-your-face burial place designed to keep people aware and impressed with his power and importance in fame forever. Now people do continue to come and be impressed, but the numbers are meager compared to those who come to Bethlehem and worship. From Jerusalem, standing on the Mount of Olives looking South, Herod's Herodian still stands prominent over the horizon, while Jesus' birth cave is obscured by that lumpy church building. But nobody ever worships at Herodian. That cave in Bethlehem and that mountain fortress of Herodian set the contrast of two ways of leadership that are still with us: the way of Jesus and the way of Herod.

Herod set the leadership style of the world into which Jesus was born. At the moment in history marked by Jesus' birth and Herod's death, Rome was well established as a world empire—the dominant military and political presence of the age. Herod reproduced that power and fanfare on a smaller scale in Palestine. In some ways, he outdid Rome. Every one of his palace complexes (and he built seven of them) was larger than any the Caesars had built in Rome. It is impossible, at least for me, not to be impressed with Herod. He ruled Palestine for twenty-four years. Politically, he was able to manipulate power-hungry Rome and many factions of religious Jews.

He had the semblance of order and prosperity. He was not a religious man, but he was a very aggressive missionary for Greek and Roman culture. He promoted and supported architecture, literary works, dramatic productions, and athletic prowess, and the buildings he commissioned were absolutely stunning—amphitheaters, hippodromes, palaces, shrines, fortifications, aqueducts, homes, roads, and his crowning achievement, the rebuilt Jerusalem Temple of Solomon. Even today, evidence of Herod's building projects can be seen throughout Palestine and Israel.

Here is the astounding thing. Jesus ignored the whole business. Jesus spent his life walking on roads and through towns dominated by Herod's palaces, Herod's buildings, and policies that were shaped by Herod's power and the mercy of Herod's whims, and Jesus never once gave Herod the time of day.

We may find this situation still more intriguing when we realize that Jesus had virtually the same agenda that Herod did. Jesus had set out to establish a comprehensive government that would shape the behavior and capture the imaginations of all the people of the world. He had his eyes on the world. God so loved the world . . . Go into all the world . . . Jesus launched his public ministry by saying the times were fulfilled and the Kingdom of Heaven was at hand.

When Jesus used the word kingdom, and he did use it repeatedly and predominantly, he was speaking in the largest and most comprehensive terms available to him. Nothing we do or feel or say is excluded from the kingdom. This is God's kingdom. Every one of your personal thoughts, actions, and feelings, yes—but also the stock market in New York, the famine in Africa, your first grandchild who was born last night, the poverty in India, the hate and the violence in Kosovo and Belfast, the abortions in Dallas, the Wednesday night prayer meeting in Richmond, the bank mergers being negotiated in Toronto, Mexican migrants picking avocados in California, everything. Absolutely everything large and small.

What I want you to get a feel for is that Jesus is working on a large scale. The largest scale imaginable. He is out-Heroding Herod in his imagination. Jesus believes that his work is to establish the kingdom on earth beginning in Palestine but not confined to Palestine. He began his work in a manger, and it continues in our hearts. "Thy Kingdom come. Thy will be done. . . . Forever and forever, Amen."[3]

Today you may well hear the call and the vision. But, the reality of life tomorrow and the forces of the Evil One will attempt to blur your vision, dull your call, and deplete your sense of excellence. Sin will discourage you. It discouraged Moses. He began to grow weary. He approached God and said: I want out, I am finished—I can't lead. These people are whiners and complainers. I am not making a difference! Dear God, what will distinguish me from all other people on the face of the earth? How will I find your brand of leadership?

The answer is an invitation to see God's glory. Moses ascended the mountain often and abandoned the ordinary. Others noticed. He was a distinctive leader and his brand of leadership made a difference. If you are not sure, ask the Israelites!

When you see a vision of greatness *and* stay in the presence of God, you glow! You are distinctive, building and delivering a leadership brand that matters! Today, I want you to see the call to distinctive leadership and I want you to see the power of the one who issues the call! It is his power that will make your brand of leadership matter. I pray for you to see a vision for yourself, for your family, for your church, and for your business of excellence and greatness!

The world needs people of vision and faith. You can see it. You are the new clergy of today's world—living and leading in homes, churches, and the marketplace. Your vision must articulate that right and wrong exist. It must proclaim that honesty and integrity are to be held in high regard. It should strongly espouse that holiness and purity are virtues.

Stay in the presence of God to care for the needy; to right that which is wrong; to release the oppressed; to commit your lives to God and your families; to have the courage to defend sacred values and the willingness to sacrifice for them. Remember, ordinary visions and ordinary faith produce ordinary lives. But visions of greatness and great faithfulness will cause you to shine.

Appendix A

WORKSHEET TABLE OF CONTENTS

WORKSHEET 1 Climbing New Towers: Environmental Analysis, Part I (see pages 76–77)		
Top 5 Positions	Internal and External Forces	
	Positive	Negative
1.		
2.		
3.		
4.		
5.		

WORKSHEET 2 Climbing New Towers: Environmental Analysis, Part II (see page 77)		
Top 5 Positions	Conclusions from Analysis	Action Items
1.		
2.		
3.		
4.		
5.		

WORKSHEET 3 Walking Where Others Walk (see page 79)	
Switching Places With . . . (Write Names Below)	Lessons Learned Write Down What You See . . .
1.	
2.	
3.	
4.	
5.	

WORKSHEET 4
A Look in the Mirror, Part I (see page 82)

Respondent: *Your friend has asked that you provide feedback relative to the leadership position listed in the box below. Please focus only on behaviors that will be helpful to this person in his or her capacity as leader noted in the box below. Each of your comments should be intended to help this person become a better leader. Your comments should be truthful and seasoned with grace.*

Position:_____

1. What behaviors would you like to see me practice more?

   _____
   _____
   _____
   _____

2. What behaviors would you like to see me practice less?

   _____
   _____
   _____
   _____

3. What behaviors would you like to see me continue?

   _____
   _____
   _____
   _____

Additional Comments:

   _____
   _____
   _____
   _____
   _____

WORKSHEET 5
A Look in the Mirror, Part II
(see pages 83–4)

Position: _____

A. List the top three areas you would like to improve upon.

    1. _____

    2. _____

    3. _____

B. For each of your identified areas of improvement, please write down why you chose it.

    1. _____

    _____

    _____

    2. _____

    _____

    _____

    3. _____

    _____

    _____

C. Write down several action items for each area you listed above.

    1. _____

    _____

    _____

    2. _____

    _____

    _____

    3. _____

    _____

    _____

WORKSHEET 6
Journey Line (see page 84)

Directions: *Represent the major markers of your life's journey on the chart provided below. Focus on emotional highs and lows relative to major events, decisions, and poignant times in your life. Begin your line at birth and end the line as of today.*

Birth ⟵————————————————————⟶ Today

+

Neutral

−

WORKSHEET 7
Mission Statement Development (see page 93)

Directions: *Use this worksheet to help you identify important elements that need to be included in your mission statement. The questions on the left side of the table should result in responses that can be recorded on the right side of the table. Use your responses to the questions to provide an inventory of thoughts/ideas needed to write your mission statement.*

Position No. & Description: _____

Issues/Questions to Consider	Answer Inventory
1. Who are you? What is your fundamental reason for existence? What business are you in? Why are you organized? What task have you been designed to fulfill?	
2. What are you good at? What are your distinctive passions and competencies (math, science, technology, language, history, business, woodworking, hospitality, etc.)?	
3. What is your current and desired scope of influence? How might you best strengthen your influence? What would the end of this journey look like if you could paint a definitive word picture?	
4. What are some ultimate goals for this position of influence? How can you measure success in this position?	

WORKSHEET 8	
Overall Goals and Objectives	
(see page 94)	

Position No. and Description: _____

Goals	Action Items
1.	1.
	2.
	3.
2.	1.
	2.
	3.
3.	1.
	2.
	3.
4.	1.
	2.
	3.
5.	1.
	2.
	3.

Directions: *Use this worksheet to help you identify what your ideal day would look like for your chosen position of focus. Use big ideas and thoughts to describe your day. Talk about interactions, events, people, outcomes. Let your right brain dominate this exercise. Please don't create a technical list of things that would be observed. The "Aha" is in the rendering!*

Position No. & Description: _____

Issues/Questions to Consider	Answer Inventory
1. What would the physical location look like?	1.
	2.
	3.
2. With whom would you be interacting? How would you describe them? What would the context of the interactions be?	1.
	2.
	3.
3. What type of culture would exist for you in this position? What values would be important? What behaviors would be prevalent?	1.
	2.
	3.
4. What types of things would you work on during the day? Give an example of a major accomplishment that would be celebrated.	1.
	2.
	3.
5. What would be the results of a really good day? Week? Month? Year? Lifetime?	1.
	2.
	3.

WORKSHEET 10
Looking Back: A Two-Year Review (see page 99)

Directions: *Use this worksheet to write a magazine article that "looks back" from two years in the future. The article should review you, your leadership style, and your major accomplishments as leader over a two-year period. Again, don't be technical. Write this article as a human interest story about you and your leadership.*

Position No. & Description: _____

_____

_____

_____

_____

_____

_____

_____

_____

_____

_____

_____

_____

_____

_____

_____

_____

_____

_____

_____

_____

_____

_____

_____

Appendix B

Note: *This appendix is intended to be used as an example for those who might benefit. The first section is a prayer that my wife and I have for our children. The second section is our family mission statement. The third section displays our core values and principles.*

To Our Children

We pray, as your Mommy and Daddy,
that you might be encouraged in heart,
and united in love, so that you may have
the full riches of complete understanding,
knowing the mystery of God, namely Christ,
in whom are hidden all the treasures
of wisdom and knowledge.
(Col. 2:2)

Lytle Family Mission Statement

To make our family a harbor of God's love
and a beacon of God's hope for all who come our way.
(Ps. 6:8, Matt. 5:13, Matt. 28:18–20)

Lytle Family Principles

To fulfill our mission as God's family, we will:

1. Honor God—believing fully in him and his son, Jesus Christ, and the Holy Spirit—for without faith it is impossible to please God (Heb. 11:6).
2. Be Passionate—loving God with all our heart, souls, minds, and strengths and loving our neighbors as ourselves (Deut. 6:4, Matt. 22:37, 2 Cor. 3:18).
3. Be Purposive—for narrow is the way and few there be that find it (Matt. 7:14).

4. Keep the Ten Commandments—not turning to the right or to the left so that our children and their children after them may fear the Lord and enjoy long life (Deut. 5:29, 6:3).

5. Be Holy—for without holiness, no one will see God (Matt. 5:8).

6. Be Prayerful—in everything, with thanksgiving in our hearts, we will make our requests known to God and his peace which transcends all understanding will guard our hearts and minds (Phil. 4:6).

7. Be Givers—in everything, honoring God with our firstfruits, giving in proportion to our blessings from the Lord (Deut. 16:17).

8. Be Servant Leaders—believing that leadership is a divine appointment which calls us to point all people to Christ (John 15:16, Matt. 28:18–20).

9. Honor one another above ourselves—knowing that God has placed us in this family and given us Lytle Power (Rom. 12:10).

10. Be Extraordinary—believing that it is a sin to be ordinary (1 Peter 2:8–9).

Endnotes

Introduction

1. John 15:16.
2. 1 Peter 2:9–10.

Chapter One—The Trouble with Generic

1. Michael Spencer, "The Coming Evangelical Collapse," *Christian Science Monitor*, March 10, 2009, http://www.csmonitor.com/Commentary/Opinion/2009/0310/p09s01-coop.html.
2. Ephesians 4:1.
3. Isaiah 40:4–5.
4. Jim McGuiggen, "Hope: Something Good Is Coming" (cassette tape series, 1970s).
5. Bruce Buskirk and Molly Lavik, *Entrepreneurial Marketing: Real Stories and Survival Strategies* (Mason, Ohio: Thomson-Southwestern, 2004).
6. Genesis 12:2.
7. Exodus 19:5.
8. 1 Chronicles 17:8.
9. 1 Samuel 12:22.
10. Exodus 33:16.
11. Exodus 33:17–18.
12. Exodus 34: 6–7.
13. Romans 2:29.
14. Prentice Meador, "A Fork in the Road," Sunday evening sermon, Prestoncrest Church of Christ, June 5, 2005.
15. Jim Collins, *Good To Great: Why Some Companies Make the Leap . . . and Others Don't.* (New York: HarperCollins, 2001), 1.
16. Mel Antonen, "Slugger Focus: Higher Power," *USA Today*, March 31, 2009, 1C.
17. John Wooden with Steve Jamison, *Wooden: A Lifetime of Observations and Reflections On and Off the Court* (New York: Contemporary Books, McGraw-Hill, 1997), 52.
18. Geoffrey Colvin, "What It Takes to Be Great," *Fortune*, October 30, 2006, 93.
19. Ibid., 94.
20. 1 Timothy 4:12.
21. Ronald W. Reagan, *A Legacy Remembered*, A&E Television, The History Channel, 2002.
22. Ibid.
23. Ibid.
24. Charles Osgood, "Pretty Good," quoted in Rafe Esquith's *There Are No Shortcuts* (New York: Anchor, 2004), 55–56.
25. Matthew 25:14–30.

Chapter Two—Brand Killer Number One: The Voice of the Crowd

1. Matthew 27:23–24.

2. Leviticus 5:1.
3. Exodus 32:22–24.
4. Exodus 32:25.
5. Genesis 3:1–4.
6. I believe this episode aired sometime in the 1980s, but I cannot find the exact record. The principle, however, is borne out in a 2002 study conducted at Victoria University in New Zealand, which similarly divided two groups of college students into groups. Half the students thought they were drinking alcohol; none were. The participants who thought they were intoxicated "acted drunk." The results of the study were published by Seema Assefi and Maryanne Garry in "Absolut® Memory Distortions: Alcohol Placebos Influence the Misinformation Effect," *Psychological Science*, 14.1 (2003), 77–80. You can read the summarizing press release on the Web site for the Association for Psychological Science, http://www.psychologicalscience.org/media/releases/2002/pr021224.cfm.
7. Terrence Deal and Lea Bolman, *Leading with Soul: An Uncommon Journey of Spirit* (New York: John Wiley & Sons, 2001).
8. John 5:39–40.
9. 1 Peter 1:18–21, 2:6.
10. John 5:44.
11. John 12:43.
12. Romans 12:2.

Chapter Three—Brand Killer Number Two: The Opponent

1. George Barna, *Revolutionary Parenting: What the Research Shows Really Works* (Ventura, CA: BarnaBooks, 2007).
2. C. S. Lewis, *The Screwtape Letters* (New York: HarperCollins Publishers, 2002), 4.
3. Ibid., 31–32.
4. *Advance Data from Vital Health and Statistics*, Number 362 (2005), publication by the U.S. Center for Disease Control, www.cdc.gov/nchs/data/ad/ad362.pdf.
5. Ibid.
6. Ibid.
7. "Facts on Induced Abortion in the United Sates," Guttmacher Institute, July 2008, www.guttmacher.org/pubs/fb_induced_abortion.html.
8. Ibid.
9. Robert S. Greenberger, "Supreme Court Overturns Itself on Sodomy Law," *The Wall Street Journal*, June 27, 2003, A4.
10. U.S. Census Bureau, http://www.census.gov/main/www/a2z/M and http://www.census.gov/population/www/socdemo/grandparents.html.
11. *Church and Family* (Searcy, AR: Harding University Press, 2002).
12. Ibid.
13. Ibid.
14. Ibid.
15. Ibid.
16. Ibid.

17. Gary Strauss, "TV Sex: Uncut, unavoidable," *USA Today*, January 20, 2010, 1D.

18. *Family Research Council*, "Planned Parenthood Report Oversexualizes Ten-Year-Olds, Undermines Parental Authority," http://www.frc.org/pressrelease/planned-parent-hood-report-oversexualizes-ten-year-olds-undermines-parental-authority, February 9, 2010.

19. *Family Research Council*. "FRC Pledges to Oppose President's Proposals to Sexualize the Military, Socialize Child Care and Penalize Married Couples," http://www.frc.org/pressrelease/frc-pledges-to-oppose-presidents-proposals-to--sexualize-the-military-socialize-child-care-and-penalize-married-couples, January 27, 2010.

20. *Family Research Council*. "FRC Statement on New Policy Requiring Military Bases to Carry 'Morning After' Pill," http://www.frc.org/pressrelease/frc-statement-on-new-policy-requiring-military-bases-to-carry-morning-after-pill-, February 5, 2010.

21. *Freedom Forum*, "Phallic art spurs censorship debate," November 16, 2001, http://www.mediastudies.org/templates/document.asp?documentID=15381.

22. Charisse Jones, "Poll: Young adults back gay marriages," *USA Today*, August 11, 2003, 1D.

23. James Dobson, *Family News*, Focus on the Family, 2002.

24. Cathy Lynn Grossman, "Episcopal Church approves gay bishop," *USA Today*, August 6, 2003, 3A.

25. Cathy Lynn Grossman, "Compromise on same-sex unions approved at Episcopal meeting," *USA Today*, August 8, 2003, 2A.

26. "Editorial: At the president's pleasure: 'Safe school czar' encouraged child sex with an older man," *The Washington Times*, September 28, 2009, http://www.washingtontimes.com/news/2009/sep/28/at-the-presidents-pleasure/?source=newsletter_opinion_headlines.

27. Diana B. Henriques and Jack Healy, "Madoff Goes to Jail after Guilty Pleas," *New York Times*, March 12, 2009, http://www.nytimes.com/2009/03/13/business/13madoff.html.

28. *The Oxford Companion to the Supreme Court of the United States* (New York: Oxford University Press, 1992).

29. John 15:16.

30. 1 Peter 5:7.

31. Ephesians 2:2.

Chapter Four—When in Charge, Take Charge

1. 2 Corinthians 5:20.

2. John 17:2.

3. Philippians 2:10.

4. John 13:3.

5. John 17:2.

6. Matthew 25:23.

7. Matthew 21:12.

8. Matthew 8:5–10.

9. Matthew 21:18–19; Luke 13: 6–8.

10. Matthew 25:26.

11. Peter Ferdinand Drucker, *The Essential Drucker: The Best of Sixty Years of Peter Drucker's Essential Writings on Management* (New York: HarperCollins, 2002), quoting Bruce Rosenstein from a 2002 *USA Today* article, Money section.

12. Ed Silvoso, *Anointed for Business* (Ventura, CA: Regal Books, 2002), 47.

13. Acts 12:12–17.

14. Silvoso, 47.

15. Mark 6:55–56.

16. Silvoso, 41.

17. Genesis 12:1.

18. Genesis 22:18.

19. Genesis 45: 5.

20. Genesis 45:7.

21. Esther 4:14.

22. 1 Corinthians 12:18.

23. Kevin Lehman, *Have a New Kid by Friday: How to Change Your Child's Attitude, Behavior, and Character in 5 Days* (Grand Rapids: Baker Publishing Group, 2008), 11.

24. Marilyn Elias, "Research Indicates Real Heroes Come From Loving Families," *USA Today*, November 11, 2001, 1D.

25. Hebrews 2:14.

26. Matthew 28:18.

27. Matthew 3:17.

28. Matthew 17:5.

29. Joseph L. Badaracco, Jr., *Leading Quietly: An Unorthodox Guide to Doing the Right Thing* (Boston: Harvard Business School Publishing, 2002).

Chapter Five—What's the Big Idea?

1. Proverbs 29:18.

2. Daniel J. Boorstin, *The Discoverers* (New York: Vintage Press, 1983), 83–86.

3. Ibid.

4. Tim and Beverly LaHaye, *The Act of Marriage after 40: Making Love For Life* (Grand Rapids: Zondervan, 2000), 30.

5. Henry Mintzberg and Frances Westley, "Decision Making: It's Not What You Think," *MIT Sloan Management Review*, 42.3 (2001), 89–93.

6. Ibid.

7. Jim Collins and Jerry I. Porras, *Built to Last: Successful Habits of Visionary Companies* (New York: HarperCollins, 1994).

8. J. Robert Baum, Edwin A. Locke, and Shelley A. Kirkpatrick, "A Longitudinal Study of the Relation of Vision and Vision Communication to Venture Growth in Entrepreneurial Firms," *Journal of Applied Psychology*, 83.1 (1998), 43–54.

9. General Electric homepage, www.ge.com/company/history/edison.

10. Ibid.

11. Jack Welch with John A. Byrne, *Jack: Straight From The Gut* (New York: Warner Business, 2001), 106.

12. Chik-Fil-A homepage, www.chikfila.com/.
13. Coca-Cola homepage, www.thecoca-colacompany.com/ourcompany/index.
14. Bruce Horovitz, "Spicing Up the Rabbit Stew," *Industry Week*, January 9, 1984, 55.
15. Dean Foust, "No Overnight Success," *Business Week*, September 20, 2004, 18.
16. James P. Womack, Daniel T. Jones, and Daniel Ross, *The Machine That Changed the World* (New York: MacMillan, 1990), 26–27.
17. Jeremiah 29:11.

Chapter Six—More Than Shadows on a Cave Wall

1. David Hutchens, *Shadows of the Neanderthal: Illuminating the Beliefs That Limit Our Organizations* (Waltham, MA: Pegasus Communications, 1999).
2. Matthew 6:22–23.
3. John McPhee, *A Sense of Where You Are: Bill Bradley at Princeton* (New York: Farrar, Straus and Giroux, 1999), 27–28.
4. Les Harrison, "The Competitive Edge: Capitalizing on Change: Make Dust or Eat Dust," *Success Strategies*, April 1995, 35.
5. Noel Tichy and Stratford Sherman, *Control Your Destiny or Someone Else Will* (New York: HarperCollins, 2001), 28.
6. Jim Collins, *Good to Great: Why Some Companies Make the Leap . . . And Others Don't* (New York: HarperCollins, 2001), 88.
7. Ibid.
8. Lee G. Bolman and Terrence E. Deal, *Reframing Organizations: Artistry, Choice, and Leadership* (San Francisco: Jossey-Bass, 1997), 5.
9. Proverbs 19:2.
10. Proverbs 14:8.
11. Proverbs 16:22.
12. Philippians 3:8.
13. Mark 1:22.
14. Ecclesiastes 7:21.
15. Exodus 4:10.
16. Exodus 4:14.
17. Proverbs 15:31.
18. Fred Smith, "The care and feeding of critics," *Christianity Today*, Winter 1995, 29–35.
19. Cresta Humphries and Jack Griggs, "Accepting Criticism and Advice," compilation from Proverbs, *The Living Bible*, selected and edited by the authors in the College of Business Administration at Abilene Christian University. Quote references, in order, are as follows: 26:12; 12:18; 11:2; 10:17; 23:12; 12:15; 12:1; 20:5; 12:14; 28:13; 12:26; 27:6; 20:18; 19:20; 27:9.
20. Fernando Bartolome and John Weeks, "Find the Gold in Toxic Feedback," *Harvard Business Review*, April 2007, 24.
21. Noel Tichy, *The Cycle of Leadership* (New York: HarperCollins, 2004).
22. *Focus on the Family* magazine, May 2005, 5.
23. Matthew 6:6–9.
24. Colossians 4:2, 1 Corinthians 7:5.

25. Mark 14:38, Luke 22:40.

26. Mark 9:29, James 5:16, Matthew 21:22, Romans 15:31.

27. Philippians 1:9, Ephesians 1:18, Ephesians 3:16, John 14–17.

28. Matthew 6:22.

29. Matthew 23:16–24.

Chapter Seven—Drafting the Vision

1. Paul W. Powell, *Getting the Lead Out of Leadership: Principles of Leadership for the Church Today* (Tyler: Paul Powell, 1997), 19–20.

2. Matthew 8:28–29.

3. Deuteronomy 6:6–7.

4. Lewis Carroll, *Alice's Adventures in Wonderland* (New York: Penguin Classics, 2007), 68.

5. Noel Tichy, *The Cycle of Leadership* (New York: HarperCollins, 2004), 74.

6. Ibid, 90.

7. Tichy, *The Cycle of Leadership*.

Chapter Eight—Power In

1. Vaclav Havel, *Summer Meditations* (New York: Alfred A. Knopf, 1992), 5.

2. Ibid.

3. Noel M. Tichy, "Getting the Power Equation Right," *Executive Forum*, Summer 2003, 32.

4. Blaine Lee, *The Power Principle: Influence with Honor* (New York: Simon & Schuster, 1997), 7.

5. John W. Gardner, *Leadership and Power* (Washington, D.C.: Independent Sector, 1986), 3.

6. Luke 3:22.

7. John 17:1ff.

8. John 17:4.

9. Luke 4:14.

10. Luke 6:19.

11. Luke 24:49.

12. John 3:34; 17:11; Acts 1:8; Romans 8:16, 1:16, 15:13; 1 Corinthians 6:14; Ephesians 1:19; Colossians 1:11; 2 Timothy 1:7; Hebrews 7:16; 1 Peter 1:5; 2 Peter 1:3; 1 John 4:4; 1 Corinthians 15:15ff; Isaiah 53:2.

13. 1 Corinthians 15:15ff.

14. Isaiah 53:2.

15. John 11:48.

16. Lee, 8.

17. Ibid, 15–16.

18. John 13:3.

19. 1 Samuel 10:6.

20. 1 Samuel 16:13.

21. 1 Chronicles 29:11–12.

22. Job 27:11.

23. Exodus 32:11.

24. 1 Samuel 16:13.

25. 2 Chronicles 20:6.
26. Job 9:4–5.
27. Psalm 89:13.
28. Luke 4:14.
29. Luke 10:19.
30. Acts 1:8.

Chapter Nine—Power Up

1. Henry Cloud, *Things You Simply Must Do to Succeed in Love and Life* (Brentwood, TN: Integrity Publishers, 2004), 18.
2. John 14:28.
3. John 15:20.
4. John 14:31.
5. Mark 7:10.
6. Luke 9:48.
7. James 4:10.
8. Jim Collins, *Good to Great: Why Some Companies Make the Leap . . . and Others Don't* (New York: HarperCollins, 2001), 21.
9. Ibid, 36.
10. John 10:11ff.
11. John 17:2.
12. Matthew 5:3.
13. Matthew 25:21.
14. 1 Corinthians 4:2.
15. Luke 2:52.
16. Luke 4ff.
17. John 8:29.
18. John 14:23–24.
19. 1 Samuel 15:22.

Chapter Ten—Power On

1. Exodus 33:12.
2. Exodus 33:13.
3. Exodus 33:14.
4. Exodus 33:15–16.
5. Exodus 33:17.
6. Exodus 33:18.
7. Exodus 33:19–20, 34:5–7.
8. Exodus 34:29.
9. Exodus 34:34–35.
10. John 17:1–5.
11. Matthew 17:2.
12. 2 Corinthians 3:13.
13. 2 Corinthians 3:18.

14. Colossians 2:2.
15. Ephesians 1:17.
16. Colossians 1:27.

Chapter Eleven—Intellectual Bandwidth

1. Matthew 22:29.
2. Luke 2:47.
3. Matthew 7:28.
4. John 6:53.
5. John 6:68.
6. 1 Corinthians 8:1–3.
7. Luke 18:10–14.
8. Matthew 23:12.
9. Psalm 78:72.
10. Noel Tichy with Nancy Cardwell, *The Cycle of Leadership* (New York: HarperCollins, 2004), xxii.

Chapter Twelve—A Healthy Heart

1. Matthew 5:8.
2. Matthew 22:37.
3. Luke 12:34.
4. Mark 5:34.
5. Luke 7:13.
6. John 11:33–35.
7. Matthew 23:37–38.
8. John 13:1–5.
9. 1 Samuel 16:7.
10. 2 Samuel 12:7–13.
11. 2 Chronicles 16:9.
12. Daniel Goleman, *Emotional Intelligence* (New York: Bantam, 1995).
13. 2 Samuel 12:8.

Chapter Thirteen—Moral Character, Edge, and Faith

1. Noel M. Tichy, and Andrew R. McGill, *The Ethical Challenge: How to Lead with Unyielding Integrity* (San Francisco: Jossey-Bass, 2003), 73.
2. Ibid.
3. Ibid, 68.
4. *Reinventing the CEO*. New York: Korn/Ferry International and Columbia University Graduate School of Business, 1989, 41.
5. Donald T. Phillips, *Lincoln on Leadership: Executive Strategies for Tough Times* (New York: Warner Books, 1992).
6. Jayne O'Donnell and Greg Farrell, "Business scandals prompt look into personal lives: Some executives facing legal trouble also hit marital rocks," *USA Today,* November 5, 2004, B:1–2.

7. Ibid.
8. Ibid.
9. Daniel 6:4.
10. James 1:18.
11. *USA Today*, December 3, 2004, 13C.
12. Josh Graves, "I will always call him Coach," Oklahoma Christian University, Alumni Newsletter, 2007.
13. Matthew 5:33–37.
14. Titus 1:5ff.
15. John 8:32.
16. Noel Tichy, *The Cycle of Leadership* (New York: HarperCollins, 2004), 94.
17. Hebrews 4:12.
18. Romans 11:22.
19. John 8:44.
20. Matthew 23ff.
21. Matthew 22:29.
22. Ephesians 3:20.
23. Hebrews 11:1.
24. Romans 4:21.
25. Luke 1:38.
26. Hebrews 11:3.
27. Hebrews 11:7.
28. Hebrews 11:8–9.
29. Tom Brokaw, *The Greatest Generation* (New York: Random House, 1998), 55.
30. Ibid, 59.
31. Ibid, 55.
32. Acts 7:23–29.
33. Paul W. Powell, *Getting the Lead Out of Leadership: Principles of Leadership for the Church Today* (Tyler: Paul Powell, 1997), 25.
34. Ibid, 29.
35. Ibid, 33.
36. Matthew 6:30.
37. Luke 5:20.
38. Luke 8:48.
39. Matthew 9:28–29.
40. Hebrews 11:6.
41. Luke 17:5.

A Final Thought

1. 1 John 2:6.
2. Hebrews 5:7.
3. Matthew 6:10, 13.